The Surgery Coach

Copyright © 2004 Joseph Casey
All rights reserved.
ISBN: 1-59457-274-7

To order additional copies, please contact us.
BookSurge, LLC
www.booksurge.com
1-866-308-6235
orders@booksurge.com

JOSEPH
CASEY

THE SURGERY COACH

MIND-BODY PREPARATION FOR FASTER, BETTER RECOVERY
(Simple, Practical Techniques for Patient, Family, and Friends)

Foreword by Judith Petry, MD, FACS

2004

The Surgery Coach

CONTENTS

	Foreword by Judith Petry, MD, FACS	xi
	Introduction	xv
1.	Your Medical Team	1
2.	Your Personal Support Team	13
3.	Hospital Risk Factors and How to Minimize Them	27
4.	Cultivating a Healing Point of View	37
5.	Breathing and Relaxation	55
6.	The Power of Words to Boost Your Healing System	65
7.	Imagery, Imagination, and Hypnotherapy	81
8.	Prayer, Forgiveness and Gratitude	97
9.	Foods and Nutritional Supplements	111
10.	The Value of Water	127
11.	Protect Your Sleep	133
12.	Music for Recovery	141
13.	A Touch of Aromatherapy	151
14.	Amazing Tools for Superior Healing	161
15.	Conclusion	167
	Appendix A: Questions to Ask Your Doctors	171
	Appendix B: What to Take to The Hospital	179
	Appendix C: Resources	181
	Appendix D: Script: Guided Imagery before Surgery	185
	Notes	191

Profound Appreciation To Those Who Encouraged Me And/or Read And Commented On The Manuscript: Newman Love, Judith Petry,md, Stan James,md, Marci Liberatore,md, Steve Holtzman,dc, Carole Grant, Jan Meredith, Nevin Schreiner, Mitch Sisskind, Larry Nagel,md, And Dralyn And Vanessa, Who Helped In Special Ways; To Healers Everywhere Making The World Safe For Integrated Mind-body Health Care; And The Charles And Frances Dudley Trust For Financial Assistance That Made It Possible To Write The Book; And To Andy Weil, Md, Who First Inspired Me To Think About Alternative Avenues Of Health In 1970; And Leonard Orr, Who Has Continued To Show Me Subtleties And Profundities In Breath And Speech Since 1974.

And To Deepak Chopra,md, Larry Dossey,md, Andrew Saul,phd, Peggy Huddleston And Steve Bhaerman For Permission To Quote Parts Of Their Work.

FOREWORD

When your surgeon says, "You need an operation", there are few of us who do not feel a deep fear of what we are about to experience. Loss of control, time away from home and work, anticipated pain and disability, and potential for permanent injury or death weigh on our minds and affect our bodies as we await the dreaded day when we must face the scalpel. More than any other aspect of modern medicine, surgery strikes fear into the hearts of patients. It is not surprising that this is so. Surgery is a well-intentioned assault upon the physical body. The results of the intervention are often miraculous, yet the method of the "fix" requires manipulating physical structure in a traumatic manner.

When I was preparing for the inevitable uterine myomectomy that I knew I must undergo to stop increasingly severe bleeding and incapacitating pain, I used many of the tools that Joe Casey describes in the following pages. I spent months exploring the spiritual meaning of my symptoms—wrote poetry, talked for hours with a wise and evolved counselor, analyzed dreams, meditated. Finally, when there was no possibility of further delay, I scheduled the surgery, consciously thanking my body for the depth of inner work, healing, and growth it had offered me through my illness. My misguided intention was to relieve my body of the physical manifestation of my emotional/spiritual imbalance. I asked my surgeon, a patient, caring, compassionate man who understood that this was my journey into which I invited him and his expertise, to remove the offending fibroma from my uterus. I proceeded to practice relaxation and visualization, listen to soothing, healing music, improve my diet, add supplements to enhance my immune system, and to pray.

When the day of surgery arrived, I was remarkably relaxed. I spoke with my anesthetist about my wishes, took my music in to the OR with me, and surrendered to my surgical team, confident, peaceful and grateful.

When I awoke in the Recovery Room, the results of my unbalanced preparation were evident. My body was in such pain and unrest that I could not imagine what had gone wrong. Pain medication relieved the incisional pain, but my body felt terrible. I was unable to sleep, and as I lay awake wondering why my careful preparation had seemed so inadequate, it occurred to me that I had lied to my body. I had been visualizing a blissful, spiritual experience, a metaphoric release of lifelong patterns of unhealthy thoughts and behavior. I had used my mind to mesmerize my body into believing that the experience of surgery would be other than a physical assault on my flesh. It was a familiar pattern in my life, focusing on the mental-spiritual aspects, suppressing the physical. I had neglected the importance of including my body in the process. My misguided intention had been to sedate my body with meditation and relaxation, rather than to assist it in facing the surgical event with its own wisdom intact.

The result was shock and surprise. My body was stunned by what had happened to it. Though I had prepared my body with healthy food and supplements, plenty of water and rest, I had not been honest about the nature of the surgical procedure. During those restless, sleepless hours after surgery, my body "told" me that I had not allowed it to prepare itself for the event. I had ignored its innate wisdom, its complex and abundant resources for confronting and healing from a physical invasion. I understood that I had treated it like a child, withholding information in order to protect it. I had not treated it as the wise, experienced and resilient organism that it is. I had, perhaps, behaved as a paternalistic surgeon towards my body, the patient.

It was a profound message for me. I was able to understand the body consciousness that regulates our heartbeats, our breathing, our blood pressure: the inborn intelligence that keeps us alive. And I saw clearly the ability of my mind to negate the importance of that physical aspect of my Being, and the results of such folly. I had treated my body as a machine, tuned it up in preparation for surgery so that it would behave as I wished it to, but I had not honored its nature. In focusing on my mind and spirit, I had relegated my body to the role of vehicle on my journey. I had removed it as an active participant, a mistake I will never make again.

That immediate postop epiphany notwithstanding, my recovery was unusually rapid and complete. The process of surgery was a remarkable education for me that integrated body, mind and spirit in a new and resonant relationship. It could not have been so had I not determined to be a full participant in the experience. We do not always know what it is we will learn when we undertake a journey. It is our willingness to be fully present to the potential that allows transformations of consciousness to occur. Surgery holds that enormous potential when engaged in completely.

As you prepare yourself, or a loved one for surgery, take heed of the invaluable information in the following pages to remove the obstacles to a successful surgery. Practice the exercises to relieve your mind of unnecessary fears; provide your body with the raw materials it requires to do its job of recovering and healing; trust in the ability of your body to respond and heal; invoke the participation of spirit; invite your loved ones to care for you; empower your surgeon and surgical team; and heal on all levels of your Being.

If the idea of being fully aware and completely involved during the time before your surgery frightens you, just browse through the preparatory tools that Joe Casey offers in this book. Practice some of the offerings that feel good to you. Notice the ones that you resist and ask yourself the reasons for that avoidance. It may be that those areas are where you need the most work. Be brave, Try something that seems difficult. If it doesn't work for you, drop it. The most important message in the following pages is that if you only try a few of the methods of getting ready for your surgery, you will still be way ahead in improving your outcome, and in learning from the extraordinary opportunity that your surgery offers.

Judith J. Petry, MD, FACS
Westminster, VT
September 2003

INTRODUCTION

"A wise man should consider that health is the greatest of human blessings, and learn how by his own thought to derive benefit from his illnesses."
Hippocrates (460 BC—377 BC), *Regimen in Health*

"The majority of alternative medicine users appear to be doing so not so much as a result of being dissatisfied with conventional medicine, but largely because they find these health care alternatives to be more congruent with their own values, beliefs, and philosophical orientations toward health and life."
J.A. Austin MD, *Journal of the American Medical Association (JAMA)*, May 20, 1998

How I Came to Write This

In 1988, my wife and my mother had major surgeries in the same month. I began to wonder what one individual, suddenly in an unfamiliar situation, could do to improve the hospital experience, maneuver around some of the risks and recover better than expected. What else, I mean, in addition to normal medical treatment. I started talking to people and reading the small amount of information available then. I had time to gather and put into use only a few of the suggestions I heard. I was able to help my wife to some extent, but I had only my presence to offer my mother, who was living 2500 miles away, dealing with serious illness and the surgery that resulted in the hastening of her death. I didn't know enough. Ever since, I've been collecting information and passing it on. Several surgeries later, I have come to realize how much all of us need the information to be in one place, easy to get at and easy to use.

As you will read, I found many studies showing clearly that surgery patients can, without going to too much trouble, do themselves a world of good. Results show improved outcomes in every category measured in such studies.

I have come to understand that medical procedures take place on many levels. On the physical-mechanical plane, doctors and nurses in modern hospitals are doing a good, often great, job. As a culture, we have allowed ourselves to pretend that's all there is to it. But it just isn't the truth. We all have feelings, emotions, worries, hopes, doubts, uncertainty and more. We know intuitively that healing happens best when we feel safe and nurtured, when our anxieties are comforted and our souls honored. Rarely, though, does a surgeon address the non-medical issues. Sometimes family practitioners do, but by and large, spiritual, psychological and emotional questions don't get a lot of time in the short interviews we have with our surgeons. They are under pressure to see more patients in less time and must deal first with the medical issues. If your doctor does take an active interest in your inner well-being, engaging with you about how you feel, consider it a big plus. If you have a doctor who recommends a course of mind-body preparation and suggests who and what might help you, consider yourself fortunate to have such an enlightened physician.

The more usual case is that we must rely on our own resources for preparation and recovery information and practice other than strictly medical. This book is intended to act as a bridge by suggesting relatively easy small actions that many people have found valuable to do for themselves, or with friends and family. Each chapter presents an idea for you to entertain. I'll try to show you how it might possibly be useful to you. I'll do my best to show you how to let this idea work for you.

I have written from the point of view of a consumer of medical services. I am not a doctor. I have, though, been around complementary and alternative wellness methods for years. I've observed a lot over the years and feel like I'm pretty much in the position of a reviewer of movies or plays, except the subject happens to be health and wellness. If you like my reviews and recommendations, you might go on and try some of the suggestions. My hope is that you see an interconnected web of ideas and practices that support each other. The more of these you try, the more benefit you will get. And the more benefit you are feeling, the better you will like what you're doing.

A rich harvest of scientific studies in the last 15 years has demonstrated the effectiveness of an array of mind-body techniques, also known as complementary wellness methods, to help bring about faster, better recoveries from surgical procedures. These practices have been shown to help surgical patients in all the ways that doctors usually measure: shorter hospital stays, lower costs, fewer complications, lower rates of infection, greater patient comfort, and less need for medication, as compared with control groups. You will learn more about these practices and the studies as we go along. And you will find improvement in ways doctors don't often measure, such as quality of life, mood, outlook and contentment.

How to Use the Book

Nowadays, about two out of three surgeries are outpatient. You go home to recover. If you have a good home environment and a good Support Team, going home can be a blessing. But do not interpret going home as an indication that your procedure is "minor." Many patients go home even after surgeries that still need to be treated as serious. Even if your surgery does fit into the category thought of as relatively "minor," it works best to think of all surgeries as important and worthy of the kind of preparation in this book. In all cases, you can help yourself by preparing mentally and emotionally. Studies of people going in for "minor" surgery show heightened heart rates and other signs of anxiety as great as patients going in for "major" surgery. One thing remains true for everyone: the better prepared you are, the better you are likely to do.

These ideas and suggestions are straightforward. The techniques are easy. I hope I've made them seem possible. There is no need for complicated rituals or practices, or a new education, to put into practice what's here. The material is intended for all of us who find ourselves in a strange and challenging situation, but don't have time to learn a whole new game. This book is designed to help you gain a feeling of being more empowered as a participant in your own healing and as a consumer of health services.

I have deliberately put in more information than one person can use all at once. Treat it as a cafeteria with many good dishes to choose from. No one is expected to take in everything. I encourage you to browse through it quickly at first, looking for what feels right to you. Let your intuition guide you. Some of you will choose one or two techniques. Others might choose more. Anything you do will improve your experience and your results. You will learn how and why to engage in the following actions:

—**Build and maintain your personal Support Team.** It is well established that patients do better when they have personal support before and after surgery. I show you, step by step, how to put together the help you need, and the reasons why.

—**Relate to and influence your medical team.** Your quality of contact with doctors, nurses, and staff has been shown to make a huge difference in outcomes. I show you how to maximize your benefit in the interviews, increasing your confidence and easing your concerns. I have included a checklist of suggested questions for your surgeon and your anesthesiologist. All you have to do is check the questions that work for you and bring the book with you to your interviews. See Appendix A.

—**Enjoy relaxation, while reducing stress and worry.** We all need to be reminded how simple it can be to take a few moments and relax. Relaxed patients do better. I give you suggestions you can do in a few minutes to change your mood and outlook. Included also is a chapter on how to get good sleep.

—**Create and attract positive healing energy.** You will easily learn and practice straightforward, proven self-healing techniques. These are specific practices to mobilize your healing system with creative imagination. You probably know about some of them. At times like this, though, many people like to be reminded of what can be done and have a few simple steps clearly presented.

—**Put language to work for you as healing statements.**

Words can influence recovery. Your words, especially your description of your present situation and your prospects, can tell a careful listener how quickly and how well you'll recover. Our words reveal and affirm our inner states. The words used by your doctors can also affect your outcome. I tell you how to get words—your own and those of your doctors—working for you to speed your recovery. As an extension, you will find chapters covering the proven effects of prayer, forgiveness and healing statements.

—**Take in appropriate healing foods, nutrients, and water.**

There's no question you can help yourself by becoming a little more selective about what you take in for a few weeks. Wide agreement exists in the natural health community about what's useful to do and not do. I provide you with this information in such a way that you easily choose your options.

—Use helpful wellness tools and resources.

There are so many possibilities: people who can help and certain items that might be useful. Choosing among them can be difficult. I've boiled the information down to a select few that I like. You can choose what to explore based on the brief explanations.

> "Everyone is a house with four rooms, a physical, a mental, an emotional and a spiritual. Most of us tend to live in one room most of the time, but unless we go into every room, every day, even if only to keep it aired, we are not a complete person."
> Indian Proverb

A Lightning Summary of What I've Learned About the Subject

These are my biases, right up front. I invite you to use these to explore your own.

—Surgery, no matter how "minor" it might seem, always involves every part of our being. It is a body-mind-heart-soul event. Surgeons today cover the body aspect very well, but are only starting to recognize mind, heart and soul. The greatest advances in healing come when we all recognize that well-being exists fully in the many layers and subtle bodies of our beings. And more, that we actually have the ability to learn to tune into and even listen attentively to more parts of ourselves

—Almost everyone and anyone can do these self-healing techniques to recover faster and better. The practices in the book can help just about everybody and anybody. It doesn't matter whether you feel fairly worry-free or feel very concerned. There's always room for improvement.

—All surgeries are serious. The sanctity of the body is invaded. A wound is created. Even though the wound is intended to further the healing process, it is nonetheless a wound. Recovery always requires thought, attention, intention and time.

—Surgeons are generally not well informed about helpful complementary wellness practices outside their scope, and sometimes have an unenthusiastic attitude about anything that doesn't come down the current medical pipeline. To be fair, they are too busy with the complex material they are already obligated to read and know. They also have reason to doubt untried modalities. Nowadays, though, more and more doctors are seeing the value of the material in this book. In the past, relatively few MDs have found time, or inclination, to study complementary and alternative wellness methods on the side. Bear in mind that we cannot reasonably expect them to tell us about, or judge, subjects they don't know. Happily, change is happening and more and more exceptions are popping up. You could get lucky, but most of us have to rely on ourselves and our personal Support Teams for complementary information and practices.

—It takes time to recover. The body has some requirements and can't be rushed. But it can be improved: how healing can be better than "normal" is the main topic of this work.

—My state of wellness is my responsibility. There is no single authority to look at to take care of me. No one has more than a piece of my unique puzzle. This probably goes for you too. A lot of it has to do with gathering your inner and outer resources and directing them consciously. We are the directors of our own wellness programs.

—My role in the medical world is customer. I make buying decisions about what they are offering for sale. So do you. You take in information and advice, then choose as best you can. Holding such a thought helps balance the traditional power of medical authority.

—It makes a lot of difference when I know what I want and care about it strongly.

—I have a fair chance of controlling how I react to circumstances and events, even if I can't *control* the event. By giving and receiving clear communication, and by being in the best, least stressed, frame of mind I can get to, I can *influence* an event. So can you.

An Important Clarification

One of the biggest concerns doctors have is that patients who become interested in complementary modalities will neglect known reliable medical treatments. Your addition of wellness practices does not and should not conflict with what your doctors want to accomplish. These "adjunct" practices support and complement the work of your doctors by helping you be in the best possible state going into surgery so that you recover faster and more wholly. The suggestions in the book are mostly in the category called "complementary wellness practices," which, according to the National Library of Medicine, are *"non-medical therapies used along with, and to assist, conventional treatments."* No conflict exists, no debate about "alternative" versus "conventional" medicine. The techniques I recommend are not "alternatives" to medical care. You do not need to choose one thing over another. I write from the assumption that you have chosen surgery as the best means to bring about your wellness. Of course, nothing in this book should be interpreted as medical advice or as a substitute for medical care. I urge you to communicate with your doctor about what you are doing for yourself.

Americans are flocking to complementary healing methods, taking our lives in our own hands in the best way. Since 1995, in every year more US health seekers have made more visits to complementary and alternative practitioners than to MDs. Here's how an article in a major nursing journal explains the connection in the specific context of surgery:

"Combining high-touch holistic therapies with high-tech surgery can contribute an enhanced balance of care to surgical patients. Proponents of blending alternative therapies with traditional health care believe that a holistic approach will help improve patient well-being. Most conventional medical practices focus on treating disease with pure science and state-of-the-art medical technology. A common sense approach to health care mandates using humanistic, simpler, less invasive, and less costly therapies as adjuncts to conventional medicine."[1]

What You Can Do Right Now

"Attention energizes and intention transforms. Whatever you put your attention on will grow stronger in your life."
Deepak Chopra

—Decide to be in charge of your own healing.
—Clearly express your intention about your surgery. How exactly do you want it to turn out?
—Imagine the best outcome possible from this procedure.
—Keep that outcome in your mind and read on.

It might help you focus if you wrote down your overall intention and your desired outcome. Read it to yourself out loud twice a day. Rewrite it whenever you like. This way, you get to have a say in deciding what happens. If you wish to let others, or fate, decide, don't write anything. Ho hum. But remember: your self-healing power is greater when you place specific attention on your desired outcome. As the great Yogi Berra once said, "You got to be careful if you don't know where you're going, because you might not get there."

If you have time to prepare for three weeks or more, consider yourself fortunate. It will give you plenty of time to get comfortable with these ideas and start practicing. If you're going in for your procedure sooner than that, you will find help, too. You will heal better and faster when you feel confident and supported by the people, the environment, and the tools you trust to help you. Together, you and I are going to organize and apply your innate self-healing abilities by pulling together your resources. In a very short while, provided you keep reading and actually do at least some of what I suggest, you'll feel more confident and at ease. I don't expect you to do everything. Just pick what appeals to you. Knowledge and information put you in a better position to choose. Let yourself feel good about what you choose to do, or not do.

A Note of Reassurance

A wise physician and surgeon, Christiane Northrup, MD, reminds us that surgery does not represent a failure, but a "healing opportunity." She points out that surgery is often the best choice under the circumstances and that agonizing over one's inability to heal a condition through "natural" methods can be a waste of time and energy. In order to alleviate some of the self-judgments many of us tend to subject ourselves to, she invites us to call the process "Creating Health through Surgery," and to view it as simply another part of the self-healing journey.2

"Courage consists of the power of self-recovery."
Ralph Waldo Emerson

CHAPTER 1
Your Medical Team

"If only you could sense how important you are to the lives of those you meet; how important you can be to people you may never even dream of. There is something of yourself that you leave at every meeting with another person. As human beings, our job in life is to help people realize how rare and valuable each one of us really is, that each of us has something that no one else has—or ever will have—something inside that is unique to all time. It's our job to encourage each other to discover that uniqueness and to provide ways of developing its expression."

Fred Rogers

This chapter will give you a look at some things you can do to make your time and experience with the doctors go better. I can't know how much time you have before your surgery, so I'm going to have to be a bit general and say things in this chapter that may not apply to you. Four out of five surgeries are scheduled more than four weeks in advance, so odds are you have plenty of time to prepare. If you have already covered some or all of this ground, feel free to skim over it.

One of the smartest things you can do for yourself is to appreciate the doctors and staff and what they are doing for you. They are bringing years of education, training and experience to your situation. And further, consider the value of appreciating the frame of mind of the surgeons and other providers. On reading the book in manuscript form, Dr. Judith Petry reminded me that this subject deserves highlighting. I can do no better than to quote part of her letter to me:

"The act of surgery is (rightfully so) an extremely stressful procedure requiring focus, preparation, attention to detail, flexibility, creativity, confidence, and a sturdy will. Surgeons and anesthesiologists live in a world with many unknowns, in which life-and-death decisions are required on short notice. The pressures of such a career choice are unimaginable to the layperson. If this reality is respected by the patient, it is not necessary to deify the doctor, only to appreciate the demands that are placed upon him or her by the very fact of the patient's need for surgery. A measure of compassion from patient to surgeon goes a long way towards cementing a healing relationship."

Getting A Second Opinion

The first and most important question to ask: "Is this surgery the best thing I can do for myself at this time?" If you are sure that it is, and you understand why you need the operation at this time, go on to the next section of this chapter. If you are not sure and don't quite know the reasons why, I suggest you get clear with your present doctor. If you feel you need a second opinion, ask. You have a right to a second opinion from another qualified specialist. Different doctors have different perspectives. They do not always agree which surgeries are necessary. A good book on the subject is *Second Opinion: The Columbia Presbyterian Guide to Surgery*, by Eric Rose, MD, chief of surgery at Columbia Presbyterian Hospital, available at most public libraries.

As to whatever condition you may have, Norman Cousins advises: "Don't defy the diagnosis. Accept it, but defy the verdict that is supposed to go with it."[1] What he means is that you don't have to accept a negative prediction about the outcome. Present-day doctors are very good at diagnosis. If you don't like the editorial comments about your future, though, get another opinion as to what course to follow, but don't buy into negative predictions. No one knows the future with absolute certainty.

How do you find out about other possibilities? Ask the nurses in your primary care doctor's office, for starters. Ask about doctors who are known to operate relatively less than others. Many doctors who perform relatively fewer operations employ other therapies to reduce the need for surgery. You might want to know what these options are. Nurses are usually knowledgeable about the preferences of many doctors, so it's likely that the surgeon's office nurses, or your Primary Care doctor and staff, will know the information you need. You can also confirm the ability of your surgeon by asking an anesthesiologist or Operating Room

Nurse who has seen him or her operate. Your own network of friends and relations can be helpful. It's amazing how many people have been having surgeries. In the US alone, there were approximately 30 million surgical procedures performed in the past year. You only hear about them when you ask. If the information doesn't come easily to you, assign a friend to track it down.

Remember, you are the primary healer. It is right for you to delegate as many tasks as possible. Always do what is the least stressful. If you start to feel anxious or overwhelmed with too much to do, ease up and ask for help.

Back surgery provides a good example of an area of medicine where opinions differ. The following statement, for example, comes from a holistic back specialist: "'If someone walks into a surgeon's office with back pain and the surgeon does an MRI (magnetic resonance imaging) and finds a herniated disk, he'll likely recommend surgery,' says Marc Darrow, MD, medical director of the Joint Rehabilitation and Sports Medical Center (www.jointrehab.com), a holistic healing center in Los Angeles. 'That's how he pays his mortgage. But studies have proven that over 50 percent of people who have disk problems do not feel any pain at all, which means that a good percentage of the pain-free population would be told they need surgery unnecessarily. In our practice the goal is to rehabilitate and restructure the body so that surgery is not even an option.'"2

Doctors disagree most about shoulder, back, or knee surgeries, but can also fairly and reasonably disagree about need or timing in many types of operations. No matter what operation you're dealing with, it's worth your time to make an effort to find out two things for yourself. First, what does at least one other learned source have to say about your situation? Second, how reliable are the outcomes? Ask your doctors to direct you to the information.

Does it surprise you to hear that surgeons believe in surgery as the best strategy for certain conditions? Of course they do; they chose this specialty and see the benefits of what they do every day. They are doing incredibly amazing things. It is possible, however, for some doctors to come to believe in surgery first, last, and in between. Just so you feel at peace with your choice, seek out another expert perspective.

The Doctor's Dilemma

Many doctors turn out to be receptive when we say clearly what additional health practices we want to do for ourselves, even if they wouldn't have considered suggesting them.

But why wouldn't they suggest complementary practices? Because they are MDs—*Medical* Doctors. They have studied *Medicine* as it is taught in *Medical* schools. They have worked hard to gain a body of knowledge and skills so large that they can barely keep up with advancing medical knowledge in their own specialties. They can often perform wonderful and amazing feats. We count on them heavily, but keep this in mind: only a few doctors in the US or UK ever study complementary health and wellness practices.

Doctors are not normally well educated in nutrition. Only a few understand energy healing, for example, or the benefits of music therapy or aromatherapy. Depending on where you live, only a small number know about much, or any, of the information in this book. But—and a big but—if you ask them about something they don't know about, their training pushes them to pretend that they do, so you might get an unreliable answer. They get away with it because we let them. They are trained to feel that they are supposed to be the gatekeepers of your body, even though they are not necessarily equipped, so they sometimes step outside of the boundaries of their knowledge. To clarify what doctors know and don't know, note this honest evaluation from leading Mind-Body Medicine pioneer, Dr. Omar Fareed of UCLA Medical School:

"Medical students are not really taught about the healing system. They are taught about disease—how to diagnose and how to treat—but they are not taught about how the body goes about treating itself. They will point to the immune system and let it go at that. But healing involves not just killing off disease germs or viruses, but the process of reconstruction and repair."[3]

The term "healing" actually makes some traditional doctors uncomfortable. Sometimes, if you're lucky and well guided, they will relate to it. But for the most part, they are trained in allopathic medicine, that is, standard hospital medicine. Many physicians, though, just don't realize that medical practice is not all there is to know about human mind-body interplay. Realistically, they are too busy to take in much knowledge beyond their immediate fields of practice. I repeat this point because it's so important to your well-being and sometimes hard to accept. Do you ask your plumber about your electrical work? It's the same house, after all.

I really don't want to make you suspicious of doctors. Almost always, they are sincere, well trained and competent, often brilliant. My hope is that you'll be comfortable trusting your surgeon once you have decided that surgery is right for you. Surgery is their business. But keep in mind that you are still the customer, in charge of your own process. We would all do well to think of our doctors, the staff, and your other helpers, as our personal team of allies. Why not consider yourself as the focalizer of your team, from whom you get information and advice when you need it. You also get to tell your team members what you need from each of them. Your true healing is in your own hands, as always.

Connecting With Your Doctors

"The way you see people is the way you treat them. And the way you treat them is what they become."
Johann von Goethe

Once you're clear about moving ahead, plan on meeting both your surgeon and the anesthesiologist as early as possible in your process, the sooner the better. You can have a big say in a lot of the specifics of your care by doing two things:

Asking questions. I've provided a list of suggested questions for each doctor, with explanations of the less obvious ones. You'll find it in Appendix A. I recommend that you check the items you want to ask, so you can have them handy at your interviews. If you can possibly work it out, especially if you are uncomfortable about asking questions, take an ally from your Support Team to every interview to listen, support, take notes and, if necessary, ask the questions. It's hard to remember everything that the doctors say, especially when there's anxiety about it, so I recommend that you record your meeting. Most people are lucky to remember the major parts of it. And do ask questions. One fascinating study recorded patient conversations with their doctors on audiotape. In interviews of 15 minutes, patients asked fewer than four questions, one of which often was "Will you validate my parking?"

Being friendly and open with everyone you meet in this process. If your doctor can see that you are a person, not just a medical problem, you're better off all around. Surgeons can sometimes refer to patients as "the kidney in 305," or "the gall bladder in 608," and think of us as our diseases rather than as our whole selves. Some surgeons see their roles as heroic: they swoop in and do their magic on a body part, and swoop right out again, without much personal contact. Surgeons are perhaps the last physicians to recognize and integrate the assistance of complementary wellness into their practices.

You can help change that. One of the best ways to improve the hospital-medical environment is to practice being more human with everyone you contact. Meet the hospital people spirit-to-spirit, person-to-person. Recognize them as whole people. Think thoughts of understanding, gratitude, and appreciation as much as you can. It's only human for them to take better care of the patients they feel they know. Be kind and courteous, yet clear and firm about what you want. And, for even more benefit, I invite you to consider feeling very lucky to have such caring, able people on your team.

Once you decide to go ahead, it's your time to gather reasons to believe that your surgery will go well and that you are in competent professional hands. Treat the doctors like valuable allies on your team. Most of them are doing very good work and deserve your respect for what they know. Medicine is a stressful and difficult job. Surgery adds pressure to perform well. Keep in mind that these are human beings doing their best. It is not a criticism to point out that there are things they don't know. Nobody knows everything. I can't emphasize enough that it's your job to manage your own care as much as possible.

The Interviews

When you are interviewing your doctors, get right to your questions in a friendly manner. Ask the questions you need to, then listen. Time is valuable to the doctors, as it is to you. But there's no need to rush, as long as you stick to the subject. Bring information they might not have, especially a list of all medications you take. Asking good questions has two positive effects:

First, the doctor knows you are an informed customer with a keen interest in your own case. Everyone pays more attention to a client with an active interest.

Second, when you have sufficient information, you can feel more comfortable and more confident. Getting your doctor to show you her or his point of view can lead to increased confidence. You can also choose to develop trust for a doctor during an interview. You can look for reasons to believe she or he can safely provide what you need.

But here's a funny wrinkle: a 2002 study of doctor-patient interviews revealed that doctors rarely allow patients to tell their stories. Doctors interrupt, on average, 20 seconds after a patient begins to talk. In spite of doctors' fears of having their ears talked off (the doctors in the study expected patients to talk for three and a half minutes), patients in the study stopped talking in just 92 seconds. There's little need for doctors to worry. The patients provided important information in those seconds. The study's lead author suggests that patients should be ready to start with a quick agenda that summarizes the issues the patient wants to know about. It gets the doctor's attention focused.4 Feel free to tell your doctor about this study.

Anesthesiology
Anesthesiologists are frequently students of the mind and consciousness. You can make good use of this by enlisting his or her support as another trusted ally in your healing. They are likely to be responsive to the idea of patients being highly suggestible in surgery and to support your use of tape or CD player with earphones (more about this in Chapters 7 and 12). They are often positioned nearest your head, so they can talk to you and perhaps help with your music. It is their business to know what state of consciousness you are in. They are also likely to be aware that use of healing tapes and music is likely to result in your body needing less anesthetic, and monitor you accordingly. It turns out that the simple act of having a meeting with your anesthesiologist lowers anxiety and improves recovery times with less pain.5

You want your anesthesiologist to have some of the same qualities as your surgeon (listed just below), with more of an emphasis of quiet support. Patients who have conversations with the anesthesiologists who will be in surgery with them have lower stress about their operations and come out with better results. It's worth making an effort to meet the anesthesiologist who will be with you during your operation, rather than a supervising MD or another doctor covering for your anesthesiologist. If that doesn't work out, you'll get a chance just before your procedure, so have your questions with you.

The Ideal Role for Your Doctor to Play

What is your ideal surgeon like? He or she has training and experience with the procedure you are going to have. Your surgeon should work in a hospital where many such surgeries have been performed. Many patients succeed in finding a caring, able, compassionate doctor who talks to them person to person. You can too. "There are many physicians who are prepared to spend time with patients, treating them with understanding and skill," concludes Norman Cousins.6 Ask everyone you know for recommendations. Your surgeon ought to have a good helping of these attributes (nobody is perfect):

Professionally skilled
Experienced with your procedure
Cheerful
Confident
Upbeat
Kind
Positive
Supportive
Able to hear what you have to say
Good attitude toward your participation
Diplomatic and humane

An interesting example of lack of communication between medical team and patients shows up in a 1990 study of preoperative anxiety about surgery. Patients were questioned before and after surgery. The surprise was that fear levels were almost as high after surgery as they had been before. First in importance to patients was fear of post-operative pain (65% before, 50% after). Second came fear of "not remaining asleep during the operation" (54% before, 28% after); then "a long wait for the operation to commence" (53% before, 41% after) and sickness and vomiting (48% before, 43% after). Judith Petry, MD, comments on the study: "The persistently high percentage of patients who still had the same fears after they had been through surgery suggests that their experience could have been improved."7.

You are entitled to a doctor with a healthy healing attitude. You don't have to be a victim of rude or condescending behavior. Watch out for anyone who threatens you with fear. It used to work, but we don't have to put up with it any more. Some doctors still frighten patients by claiming that complementary and alternative practices are dangerous. They might say that there are no studies of this or that, even when they do exist. They just haven't read them, but still want to be in power.

Doctors are in transition: they used to be the authority figures. You, the patient, had to do what they said, or else. We customers have to help retrain them in their roles, which are somewhat less grand and much more equal than they used to be. Learning from patients is a sign of an intelligent physician. Feel free to tell your doctor that you want a doctor-patient relationship that supports you participating in the healing process and in which you feel a caring attitude that lets you place your trust.

"Medicine is less scientific than we've always counted on it to be," says Dr. Herbert Benson, of Harvard Medical School. He cites with approval several sources, including Yale professor Sherwin Nuland, MD and the editor of the British Medical Journal, who agree that "no more than 15% of medical treatments are founded on reliable scientific evidence."[8] Medicine is, more realistically, a body of more or less agreed-upon strategies and methods that are believed to work better than other options. Much of what doctors actually know and do is practical stuff learned from other doctors on the job. They have to treat patients in the real world and must do the best they can under the circumstances. Muddling along has sufficed for humans for thousands of years. I am not troubled by the muddling along, which works well in practice, but by the unwarranted pair of assumptions that what they are doing is always truly "science" and that they alone know about every part of healing.

Generally, it helps to inform your doctors what other modalities you are getting help from, but a word of caution: you must first determine if they are grown-up enough to listen without judgment or attitude. If they are treating you and prescribing for you, it makes you safer if they know. The unfortunate reality is that more than seven out of every ten patients do not tell their doctors about complementary therapies they are doing because they are afraid the doctor will feel threatened and/or ridicule them.[9] Authoritative medical scorn has for centuries been one of the best weapons for preventing change and intimidating patients. Keep in mind that they have been taught to dismiss everything they have not learned in medical school. This attitude helps neither patient nor doctor, both of whom would be better served by friendly openness.

If you have a doctor who speaks negatively about your prospects or about any wellness practice you have chosen, without offering evidence and a clear explanation, ask for a full explanation. If you don't get satisfaction, find another doctor. You don't want your doctor practicing medical voodoo on you, hexing your recovery. Fear-based attitudes are bad for your health. Negative remarks about your health choices can affect your state of mind, which in turn has an effect on your outcome.

When you are facing surgery, you are in a highly suggestible state, in which all statements from doctors, nurses, and others take on heightened meaning. Every word from the doctor is, in effect, a hypnotic suggestion taken in by the patient, whose resistance to suggestion is lowered by the stress of being in front of a doctor. Even so, be as active as you can be in holding on to your center, rejecting negative comments. You didn't sign up to be hypnotized by someone who has power, but no training in, or understanding of, the real power of suggestion. And I'll say again: take a friend who can support you at your appointments and help with making a tape of the meeting.

If you are truly engaged in something the doctor believes is dangerous, or which interferes with treatment, he or she needs to explain the reasons. Reasonable evidence is valuable to you. Back and forth communication is ideal. We can do without unsupported attitude. Remember: your doctor is not necessarily in a position to tell you *everything* that might be helpful or useful to you. Accept that you will get some of what you need from other resources, as you are doing now. I emphasize again: the doctors deserve your respect for what they know how to do. In return, they can learn to appreciate what they do not know. They really do need allies who can support and complement their work, even if some of them haven't realized it yet. Your healing is a team effort.

Who Does the Healing?

The surgeon repairs obstacles to your health, but does not heal you. You do that yourself. You are the healer, the healing and the person healed. The best doctors know very well that they do not do the healing, even when their work is a necessary prerequisite for healing to occur.

Three factors most affect the process of self-healing, according to

Dr. Herbert Benson of the Harvard Mind-Body Institute, in his book *Timeless Healing*. His term for our ability to heal ourselves is "remembered wellness." The body acts on a stimulus to refer back to previous states of health in order to repair itself. It's a good way to think of the self-healing ability too often dismissed as "just the placebo effect." The factors are:

—Belief and expectancy in the patient.

—Belief and expectancy on the part of the caregiver.

—Belief and expectancy generated by a relationship between patient and caregiver.10

Dr. Benson adds a crucial element: "Studies show you'll recover more quickly if your surgeon is upbeat, confident, and kind."11 Your belief is the most important thing you have going for you. If you believe something or someone will help you, especially when your caregivers share that belief, you increase the likelihood of success.

To make this point clearer, consider one of the most fascinating of several studies about belief cited by Dr. Benson: "To see how the patients' beliefs triggered remembered wellness, take a look at Dr. Stewart Wolf's 1950 study of women who endured persistent nausea and vomiting during pregnancy. These patients swallowed small balloon-tipped tubes that, once positioned in their stomachs, allowed researchers to record the contractions associated with waves of nausea and vomiting. Then the women were given a drug they were told would cure the problem. In fact, they were given the opposite—syrup of ipecac—a substance that causes vomiting.

"Remarkably, the patients' nausea and vomiting ceased entirely and their stomach contractions, as measured through the balloons, returned to normal. Because they believed they received anti-nausea medicine, the women reversed the action of a powerful drug. Even though many of us stock our medicine cabinets and first aid kits with ipecac to bring about vomiting in case of poisoning, these pregnant women with documented stomach distress thwarted the action of a drug that should have made them even sicker. With belief alone, they cured themselves."12

If the mind can do that and other wonderful acts of self-healing, what else can happen? We're not talking about belief setting broken bones or performing triple bypasses. That's why we go to surgeons. This is about your part of the healing equation, and just how important your part is.

A Note about Medication

Tell your surgeon and anesthesiologist ALL the medications you are taking, including herbs and vitamins or other nutritional products. A lot of people forget to mention the anti-depressants or other mood pills. The information can affect your doctor's choices about your treatment and medication. Make a list and bring it with you to your meetings and to your surgery, where it will be helpful and reassuring to the nurses who get you ready. While you are at home now, write down absolutely everything you take. Don't guess. This goes for herbs and supplements as well. Whether you're taking herbal diet pills or mood enhancers, let them know. Your doctors will very likely tell you to stop taking the herbs and all but the most necessary pharmaceuticals for two weeks before surgery. They are trying to lessen the chance of an adverse drug reaction and improve your chances of safety and good recovery. You will find more detailed information on supplements in Chapter 9.

Use the checklist of questions at the end of the book, in Appendix A. Your job is to choose which questions apply to you and check them off so they'll be available to you at your meetings. Some of them will make more sense after you've been through all the chapters. Check off the questions most important to you, add your own, and take them with you to interviews. You will never be at a loss for something to ask.

And One Super-Important Note about Your Safety

The instructions given you about not eating or drinking for a directed number of hours before surgery are more important than you may realize. Follow them absolutely. Nurses hear all the time from patients who just "had" to have the morning cup of coffee, or some food ("I just couldn't make it that long."). If you take in food or drink, you risk many things: delaying your surgery, nausea during anesthesia, gross inconvenience for the surgeon and staff gathered together for you, and, not least, your life. Make a pleasure out of being a good patient in this matter.

Medical Information On the Internet

If you want to know a lot more about a specific operation, go to www.wellnessweb.com and click on the human body image, which takes you to www.preop.com. Very good information is at these sites, clearly presented. Look for others in the *Resources* section, Appendix C.

CHAPTER 2
Your Personal Support Team

"There is nothing better than the encouragement of a good friend."
Katherine Hathaway

"Flatter me, and I may not believe you. Criticize me, and I may not like you. Ignore me, and I may not forgive you. Encourage me, and I will not forget you."
William Arthur Ward

Why A Support Team?

Why do you need a Support Team? In a nutshell, you will do better, feel better and recover faster. I capitalize Support Team because I want to emphasize the value and importance. Having support lowers stress and speeds healing and recovery. Loving yourself enough to gather support brings healing closer. Your healing system, your whole being, seems to know when you are being cared for and when you are caring about and for yourself.

What does a Support Team do? Anything and everything, ranging from everyday household tasks to being with you in the hospital, looking after your interests and defending you. The job is to take care of enough of your tasks that your stress level is as low as possible. At the end of the chapter I expand your team to include healers you might be able to round up.

The biggest sources of stress for most people going into surgery, aside from the operation itself, are the most basic needs, such as cooking or taking care of kids, pets, and social obligations. We don't usually think of taking care of the everyday stuff as healing work. We ought to, though. It affects everything. When a person cannot engage in normal activities, he or she feels the stress of undone household tasks. The web that depends on those actions—family or friends—feels the stress, however seemingly small. Realizing this, everyone can act as a healer just by picking up a strand for a friend.

Having a Support Team helps reaffirm the ancient idea that a person's community is part of healing. Invite friends who are loving and optimistic to play a role on your team. This chapter spells out what the team can do and how you put one together.

Asking friends for help offers them an opportunity to be of genuine service. Just about every religion honors and promotes assisting or visiting the sick as an act of grace, a way of nurturing one's soul. The Catholic Church grants time off in purgatory for this good deed. Buddhists earn merit for it. So when you ask for help, you are giving someone a chance to do a good deed and feel good about it. It's a blessing. Don't mind the ones who don't accept. Give thanks for those who do.

Hospital patients receiving personal support do better by every measure: they experience less pain, less need for medication, lower stress, and shorter hospital stays. A study at Dartmouth Medical School showed heart patients who were in community and social groups were an astounding three times more likely to survive.1 Conversely, isolation and loneliness increase the mortality rate by 3-5 times, according to Dr. Dean Ornish.2 This is a time when it is appropriate to allow yourself to receive help.

My friend and neighbor, Stan James, MD, is a well-known orthopedic surgeon who has operated on hundreds of elite amateur and professional athletes. We were talking about why significant differences in surgical outcomes occur. He told me he was recently giving a speech and was asked to compare treating, for example, a world class athlete lower back injury and a similar injury in a Workman's Comp patient. He told the audience that when the top athletes come in, the Support Team comes too: friends, teammates, and family. The team fervently desires that he or she return to wellness as soon as possible; and wants the athlete to come to practice and watch, just to be there sharing energy. There's a feeling of belonging. The friends and family members bring their caring. They appreciate each other. The office staff and physical therapists respond to this energy. The staff is welcoming. They can't help being aware of the positive feelings, the hope and optimism coming into the office. The surgeries and recoveries usually go well.

The Workman's Comp lower back injury patient, in contrast, typically comes into the office alone and depressed. He or she is going to try to tough it out solo. Even when friends and family could come, no one has thought it important. The boss has said: "We don't want to see you until you can work." Seldom does a sense of belonging to a group come along with this patient. The office staff groans inwardly because they know how hard it's going to be. The therapists and staff can't help being pessimistic. It is well understood that Workman's Comp recoveries usually don't go as well. Support—the kind that has the patient's highest healing potential as the aim—is found again and again to play a large role in the difference. Isolation and loneliness work against healing.

The level and quality of support make as much difference in outcomes as any other factor. People who know they are part of a team, know they are cared about, know they are wanted back, and know they are still part of the group even if they can't perform now, usually have the best surgical outcomes.

You don't have to be a sports star to have a Support Team. You probably already have one, even if you don't think of it as such. When you visit the surgeon's office with an optimistic friend or two or more, you can shift the expectancy of doctor and staff so they strongly feel you are going to do well, just as you feel it. The idea is to get everyone believing in you. The more people who believe in you, the larger your aura of wellness. Bring some magic with you and it will expand. Now let's get it working for you.

Who Do You Need?

As in the other chapters, you get to choose what appeals to you and make up your own list of needs.

—Someone to help you organize, plan and support your choices from the book.

—Someone to go with you to meetings with your doctors, to take notes and help ask questions and maintain your calm, balanced state of mind.

—Someone to take you to the hospital and be with you before your operation.

—Someone to help you get settled when you come out of recovery.

—Several someones to be with you as long as you are in the hospital, or at home recovering but not completely self-sufficient. Help at home is crucial.

The best possible people for the above roles are your more sympathetic friends, reasonably calm and outgoing, with caring, nurturing qualities. Their job is to engage with hospital staff on your behalf, so they have to be willing to ask questions and say, "Hey, is that supposed to happen?" Ideally, that person will have listened to the healing tape you have chosen or, perhaps, read aloud some of the guided imagery selections to you (See Chapter 7). Maybe one or more friends reads this book and collaborates with you about how to put your chosen activities into practice. Everyone should know they are there to support your healing and to avoid doing anything that takes your energy away from healing.

Your recovery period will go faster if you have few social visits that require you to speak, or even listen to casual conversation. Your energy is best directed to healing. This is true both at home and in hospital. Your team should be able to keep anyone away from you who wants to demand your attention. Nor do you need anyone nervous or fearful around you before or after. You may not believe that you are affected by the moods of others, but your body surely responds to them. Keep good energy around you. If you know already that someone's presence adds stress, find a diplomatic way of getting them a helpful role that requires their presence elsewhere. You can always have more than one helping person with you.

There's more. You may also need:

—Someone to stay with you in your room, in 2-4 hour shifts, most or all of the time, while you are in the hospital. What do they do?

—Reassure you and nurture you as you wish.

—Keep the caregivers optimistic about you by enlisting them in the reality of your excellent recovery..

—Have a list of your medications, make sure there are no errors, and question if there's a change.

—Keep you from getting steam-rolled by something the staff wants to happen that might not be in your best interest.

—Guard you against being awakened unnecessarily.

—Provide the foods you need, the tape you want to hear, the aromatherapy you want, the healing aids you've brought with you.

—Keep your energy from being drained by visitors you don't really want.

And more:

—People to clean house, put dinners in the freezer, help with driving or take care of children, take care of pets, paint the house, and so on. Make a list of the things you'd like help with and give the right task to the right person. Even better, ask someone to pull a few people together. Uncle Elmer might not do food or aromatherapy, but can take good care of your dog or drive you somewhere. Having everyday tasks handled relieves stress.

If you have enough people, shifts can be short and vary according to people's schedules. I suggest you find someone to be responsible for doling out tasks to people who can visit for a short while. Everyone can do or bring something that helps. Otherwise, people sit around and sap your strength. If they're not contributing to your healing, they should not be there.

No small children should see you in the hospital for at least a day after surgery, if you can avoid it. Mostly, they'd just as soon not, and the next day you'll feel more like it. It can distract you from healing and might frighten the children. If you are going right home, use your judgment, plan beforehand what your preference is, but minimize their presence by having a team member do something fun with them away from your room. Angry or negative folks? Keep them busy somewhere else. This is your time to heal, not to be socially obligated. Ask for help in controlling visitors. You need to be free of having to put out energy at this time. Let your helpers and the healers come forth.

You also could use:

—Several people who agree to think of you positively, pray for you, meditate on your healing, or whatever they like, around the time of your surgery. As many as you like from wherever they are. No travel time needed. See Chapter 8 for a full explanation of the value of prayer. Every little bit helps, so encourage even a commitment of a couple of minutes. Ask a friend to call and/or email your prayer (or positive thought) team to remind them of when your procedure is happening.

—As many talented healers as you can manage. Specifics below, near the end of the chapter.

Healing Circles

Some of the same people might want to have a healing circle for you.

This could be anything you feel good about, from a few friends gathering around you for a few minutes of healing intention to a more formal ritual. You don't need a formal plan, but it's OK to have one. One possibility: each participant brings a message, a prayer, to read or say aloud. We often bring a bowl of sand (or salt) and each wellwisher lights a small candle to represent a healing idea, spoken aloud, and puts it in the sand. Before your surgery, the emphasis ought to be on relieving stress and worry, plus holding a positive thought about your surgery. For healing circles after the operation, the emphasis shifts to healing the physical trauma and the emotional wear and tear from the whole adventure. Keep in mind that you are deserving of attention and care at this time. Your job is to be receptive. Allow it in.

What Do You Need?

This list sort of dovetails with the "who do you need" list. I want to make sure everything is emphasized. Feel free to improvise:

—To feel support, optimism, caring during all your pre-surgery hospital contacts.

—To be protected from events or people that could harm you, upset you, or lower your energy.

—To be protected against incorrect medications and dosages.

—To have a friendly, comforting presence near you.

—To have as much support as possible for your recovery and healing.

—To have help while you're in the hospital and when you've just come home, whether it's taking care of children, doing meals, or being with you.

—To receive healing touch, massage, and foot massage.

Who do you ask? To start with, ask people who feel like they can support your healing. Lots of people can be loving and caring when they are invited to be. Choose from:

—Your close and extended family.

—Friends. Give them a chance to show they care.

—Groups you are a member of: social, church, work, sports team, for example. Ask the leaders to connect you to loving people. Churches are rediscovering their mission as healers.

—Anyone who has had a similar surgery.

—Ask the surgeon's nurses if they know of people who help in recovery.

—Friends who practice Reiki or Touch Therapy or foot reflexology, or who know someone who does who might come to see you.

Find the right task for the right person. Some people do dishes but not bedside care, massage but not cooking. How do you get people to help? By asking. By having conversations with friends about the ideas in this chapter and the rest of the book. What would they want to have happen for them? Would they do that with you? Who else might? Beyond that, could you or a few friends organize a mutual support circle, agreeing to help each other?

Prayers and Other Good Thoughts for You

A rigorous study of 990 patients in a Coronary Care Unit at Duke Medical showed that those in the group prayed for by strangers far away had better scores in a 4-week evaluation than those not prayed for. The patients had no knowledge of the prayers, so their belief did not play a part. The authors conclude: "This result suggests that prayer may be an effective adjunct to standard medical care."[3] This is really big news. You'll find more reasons to consider prayer "as an adjunct" in Chapter 8.

How much do studies of prayer matter? Not much, to people who are already in the habit, but possibly helpful for others. If it feels right to you, go ahead and do it. Since it does seem to be helpful in a manner not easily measured, with no risk of harm, why not allow yourself to receive healing prayer from other compassionate souls? The most comfortable feeling comes when you've got a group of friendly people you know and love. But since there is evidence that even non-local prayer from strangers appears to have a good effect, it seems like a no-lose situation, with much to gain. If you are not comfortable with prayer, think of this simply as people holding friendly, positive, healing thoughts and intent. It need not be religious.

In these wonderful times, you can even sign up on the Internet and be connected to worldwide networks of healing energy. I've listed some sites to choose from in *Resources*. It is inspiring and reassuring to perceive a world with an abundance of loving people who have time and energy to pray for others. Let's have more of it. Still, my personal belief is that even though prayer appears to have a good effect when it comes from strangers (the patients not knowing they are being prayed for), it works even better when you know it's happening and you feel the connection. When you allow the personal factors in, it feels better than the merely clinical. It does no harm and has a possible benefit. Why not?

To give you one more look at how medical science is viewing these once-unusual practices: a couple of years ago, researchers reviewed 23 studies of non-local healing, involving 2774 patients. Five of the trials examined prayer as the distant healing intervention, 11 assessed non-contact Therapeutic Touch, and 7 studied other forms of distant healing. Of the 23 studies, 13 (57%) yielded statistically significant treatment effects, 9 showed no effect over control interventions, and 1 showed a negative effect.4 Wouldn't you say that any practice that had been shown, scientifically, to have better than 50-50 odds of improving your outcome is worth considering, even going to a little trouble to arrange?

Emotional Support

You can count on it: the prospect of surgery concentrates the emotions. "Illness is a type of loss that brings on the grief process," writes John Travis, MD, one of the pioneers of mind-body medicine. He goes on to say: "Few of us recognize how powerful are the interconnections of mind, body, and spirit. It is natural to feel scared, insecure, or even worthless when your body is wounded in some way. Accepting ourselves as hurting human beings, who are still basically okay, is an essential first step to full healing." 5

We are all presented with an opportunity to move through some version of the classic stages when we come up against major stuff: Denial, Anger, Bargaining, Sadness, and Acceptance. People who do well in surgery have usually worked their ways up this scale by acknowledging and allowing the feelings as they come up. Acceptance helps the work of the doctors. How do you get there? First, read the rest of this book. The text is sequenced so you will very likely wind up feeling better and better as you move on from here.

Second, locate a friend with sound emotional intelligence. Talk over the five stages and evaluate where you are. Let yourself grieve consciously over your situation, realizing that even a "minor" operation can bring up blame, self-blame, and various anxious feelings. You might say we all have a bit of grieving to do over not being perfect. If no one seems right, call the hospital and ask for pastoral care or the integrative medicine unit. A wonderful book about the emotional aspects of healing is Regina Sara Ryan's *After Surgery, Illness, Trauma*.

Christiane Northrup, MD suggests a healing ceremony or ritual in which you say kind words to the part of the body being repaired. If a part is being removed, give thanks to that part and say goodbye kindly. "When an organ or cell tissue is removed," she writes, "and the body messages associated with it are not acknowledged or processed. Then part of our energy will remain in the past like an unpaid account, a part of our unfinished business."[6] A good friend can help you create a mini-ritual and encourage you in allowing the material to emerge from under the surface.

Touch Therapy

Any well-intentioned person with a conscious intention to help or heal can do touch therapy. It used to be called "laying on of hands," one of the most ancient healing practices, now having a revival. Kind and reassuring touch reduces anxiety, improves mood and provides comfort and caring. You'll also find that many nurses have had training in touch, and enjoy doing it, in part because it allows them a form of caregiving that feels good. Yes, trained healers do get better and more consistent results, but I want to emphasize that every caring person's touch is inherently healing. We all have the power in ourselves, in our hands, to offer energy that helps others to heal themselves. Healing energy is available to every person on earth. We don't need degrees or licenses or qualifications to offer loving, supportive simple human energy to another. Can you think of a friend who can just be with you while holding a healing intention, one who won't need to engage you in conversation if you are tired? Intention is the key. Often, simple hand holding will feel reassuring. Many people in our strange culture go for long periods without any touching. If you have a friend in a stressful situation, go ahead and ask if it's OK to hold his or her hand or touch a shoulder. If you are the patient, ask for it.

One study shows that trained Therapeutic Touch practitioners can have a positive effect in only 5 minutes a day, even when they don't actually touch the patient and cannot see or be seen by the patient. The healers worked on the other side of a wall from the patients. Researchers found "a significant acceleration in the rate of wound healing as compared to the non-treated subjects.... Statistical comparisons are dominated by the complete healing of 13 of 23 treated subjects vs. 0 of 21 control subjects by day 16. Placebo effects and the possible influences of suggestion and expectation of healing were eliminated by isolating the subjects from the Therapeutic Touch practitioner, by blinding them to the nature of the therapy during the study, and by the use of an independent experimenter who was blinded to the nature of the therapy."[7]

Your surgery makes a wound and it will most likely heal faster with Therapeutic Touch, Touch for Health or Reiki. Got it? In spite of the word "touch," none of these practices need involve any touching. They are often done at a distance of a few inches from the body. Most hospitals have trained people available, usually RNs. Ask your doctor or the nursing staff if you can have a treatment or two. In some hospitals, the doctor must order it. The pastoral care office is a also good place to ask. Often, they can help when the doctor won't. If it doesn't come through the hospital, then work your network. Healing touch is one of the most important things you can do for yourself before hospital and after. It is worth paying for.

To press the point in the other direction, it is well established that stress slows healing, and in particular, wound healing. This is the reason for the many methods of stress reduction, from breathing to music, I recommend throughout the book. Having a Support Team lowers stress. Not having one can increase stress levels. Healing touch, among other practices, definitely lowers stress. This excerpt from *Science Daily* speaks volumes: "Scientists investigating why wounds heal more slowly on patients who are stressed have found that psychological stress can increase the levels of some hormones in the blood. These hormones can slow the delivery of certain compounds—cytokines—to the site of the injury to start the healing process. But if the process is slowed at the beginning, the wound will take much longer to heal, posing potentially serious consequences to patients recovering from surgery. 'There is a lot in the medical literature suggesting, if possible, that a patient should not be under stress before surgery,' explained Jan Kiecolt-Glaser, professor of psychiatry and psychology at Ohio State University. 'Stress, depression and anxiety prior to surgery have all been associated with poor surgical recovery.'"[8]

I'll return to this study in Chapter 5, where we get to techniques for stress reduction. The most significant point is that almost all surgery patients have stress and anxiety before surgery, so that the norm of surgical recovery is not as good as it could and should be. Yet surgeons give little or no attention to relieving stress and anxiety before, during and after surgery. Tranquilizing medication is not an adequate substitute, although it can be enormously helpful when a patient is anxious and the process is rolling.

Massage Therapy

Trained healers and massage therapists can have a great effect. Think about who you can recruit. Who among your friends knows energy or touch healers? There's a lot of evidence that massage therapy speeds both wound healing and overall recovery, or whole-system healing. In a hospital study in England, surgical patients receiving massage therapy reported increased relaxation (98%), a sense of well-being (93%), and positive mood change (88%). Greater than two thirds of patients attributed enhanced mobility, greater energy increased participation in treatment and faster recovery to the massage therapy.9 Do those benefits sound OK to you?

Even something as apparently simple as hand massage appears to decrease psychological and physiological anxiety levels in patients having cataract surgery under local anesthesia.10 And in a publication aimed at RNs, I found the following comment:

"Tactile therapies use touch with conscious intent to help or heal. Touch can convey reassurance, comfort, and caring in a way that words cannot. Patients who received massage in an intensive care unit exhibited improvements in mood, body image, self-esteem, and levels of anxiety. Tactile nursing interventions such as massage, therefore, may provide reassurance to anxious surgical patients."11

Reiki

If you have never had a Reiki session, give yourself a treat and find yourself a Reiki practitioner ASAP. You'll be glad you did. Reiki relaxes and activates internal systems that encourage your healing system. Not only do you get to relax from the inside out; you become stronger internally, therefore better able to recover from surgery. If you can manage to have a session a few days before, and again right before your surgery, do both by all means. Your surgeon will appreciate your increased muscular relaxation. Having a session soon after surgery speeds recovery by activating the healing response. Here's an excerpt from a study of Reiki in *The Journal of Advanced Nursing:*

"Anxiety was significantly reduced after the Reiki treatment, and IgA levels were significantly raised. Blood pressure dropped significantly…Biochemical and physiological changes towards greater relaxation are suggested by these findings, and the changes in IgA levels warrant further investigation of the effect of touch therapies on immune function."[12]

Isn't that just the sort of thing we're looking for? A simple practice that lowers blood pressure and anxiety, increases immune function, doesn't hurt, is not invasive—and you get it with your clothes on. As in Therapeutic Touch, the healer's hands do not need to touch you, although many Reiki practitioners will rest their hands gently on you if you like. It's good. Go for it.

Give yourself a great gift and find a Reiki or Touch for Health or similar energy healer; a massage therapist, and anyone you like who has good energy to give you. These are very high value activities. Patients do much better with them than without. Ask your doctor if the hospital can provide one of these forms of energy work before and after surgery. After surgery, the treatments can speed healing time by relieving the stress that all procedures bring on. Ask. The more you ask, the more likely it is to be available. Hospitals rely on the evaluations they get from patients, so they are rapidly changing.

Emotional Freedom Technique (EFT)

One of the best ways to relieve pre-surgery concerns and anxiety is a process of gently tapping on certain points while saying an appropriate phrase or sentence that connects mind and body. Perhaps you know someone who can show you how to tap and where. If not, go to the web site (www.emofree.com) and learn how. Effective EFT can be done on the telephone. I do it on the phone for clients as part of the coaching process. This story explains the value:

"I had a client who was suddenly called to the hospital for some surgery on her feet that she had been waiting for. Her experiences in hospitals had always been very anxiety provoking to the extent that her anxiety was at a 10 and she was sweating.

We went through the entire EFT procedure step by step from being admitted, to the needles, to the anesthetic, to going under, to waking up post op. She was about a 10 at every step along the way and we tapped on each new anxiety as it came up. When she left, she felt calm and was not afraid to have the surgery, which was to take place the next day. She called me a few days later to explain how the surgery went. She said everything went fine. She didn't get scared the whole way through. The needles were relatively painless and she didn't get cold or sick in post op, which was the norm for her."

L.C., EFT practitioner13

Reflexology

To add one last grace note, Reflexology works, too, as researchers found when they discovered that reflexologists could direct blood flow to a particular organ, just working the points on the bottoms of the feet.14 The practical value is this: directing blood flow, during the recovery period, to the area of surgery, speeds healing. Any friend can get one of those little foot charts from the health food store and press the appropriate points that will send blood flow to the appropriate area of the body. An experienced practitioner will help even more.

I have written about many possibilities. You don't have to adopt any of them if you don't want. If you do, though, you'll be glad you did. The main idea I would like you to come away from this chapter with is that the best Support Team you can build is the one that you like, the one that satisfies your felt needs. Use these suggestions as a springboard to find the help you want.

CHAPTER 3
Hospital Risk Factors and How to Avoid Them

"A hospital is no place to be sick."
Samuel Goldwyn

Any hospital stay, even at a short-stay surgery center, puts a patient at risk. You will unquestionably fare better if you know what the risks are and take steps to protect yourself. The more prepared you are, mentally, physically, emotionally, and spiritually, the more likely you are to slide past the hazards. I will tell you the main things to look out for and how medical experts recommend you protect yourself. There are no guarantees. No one can eliminate all risk, but you *can* reduce it significantly.

The issues that hospitals are facing: staff shortages, overworked staff, germs that are becoming resistant to antibiotics, sometimes overwhelm everyone. I offer the information that follows so you will know what you are dealing with and prepare yourself appropriately. And you will know more about how to take care of yourself and get help.

As you know, hospitals are organized for the benefit and convenience of the doctors, the administrators, staff, and insurance companies. Last and least comes the patient.1 In plain English, it isn't the luxury hotel business, even though it costs more.

Each year, there at least 30 million surgeries in the US alone, up to 50 million of all possible types, according to the authors of *Surgery: A Patient's Guide from Diagnosis to Recovery,* leading authorities in Nursing. They state: "It's shocking to note that statistically, the rising number of surgeries can be attributed not to the population growth, but rather to an increase in the number of surgeons."2

It may be that you are having surgery in an outpatient surgery center. Lots of operations don't happen in hospitals. Bear in mind that just because your procedure is outpatient doesn't mean it is insignificant or free of risk. Most of the same preparations still apply. All surgeries need to be taken seriously. Preparing well is always the best course.

Hospital Infections

Bacteria thrive everywhere in the hospital and can spread through contaminated hands or rubber gloves of hospital workers, or through food, medical instruments, or the coughing and sneezing of staff or other patients. These infections have a fancy word to describe them: doctors call them *nosocomial infections* (so you won't understand, naturally). You might think that it's something that you can only get in a country called Nosocomia. No such luck. It means "hospital-caused."3

Bacteria responsible for infections can spread from patient to patient through contaminated hands of health care workers. The risk of spreading the infection could be considerably reduced by adherence to simple hand washing, or even better, the new disinfecting wipes, which you can buy at any pharmacy. I recommend that you bring some along in your hospital kit. You can offer them in a friendly way to nurses and staff.

Infection prevention rates high on the list of questions to ask your surgeon. I cannot emphasize enough how important the relationship between you and your doctor is. The more of a real person you are to her or him, the better you know each other, the better off you are. I'll say again: put a check mark next to the questions in Appendix A that you want to ask. Take the book to all your doctor meetings. You will feel more empowered.

What to Do to Prevent Hospital Infection

A few basic strategies to lower risk of infection can help keep you from being one of those statistics. No method is perfect. Nothing destroys every germ, but you can improve your odds quite a bit. I'll be going over these, with more explanation, in other chapters. The best defense is always to build your immune strength and personal vitality. The rest of the book shows several ways to do so right now.

—Encourage hand cleansing and glove changing as much as you can. Be friendly and clear. The information supports you, but it doesn't work to be heavy-handed with the nurses. Do your best with good grace, humor, and the fostering of teamwork. A relay of friends from your Support Team should be with you, as much as possible, to help protect you. Maybe you could find or make a cartoon that makes the point without being annoying. A friend can sometimes help in a way that doesn't harm your reputation with staff.

—Build your immune system strength in the weeks before your procedure. Infection fails to thrive in a strong immune system. This is the underlying theme of nearly every chapter of the book. Stress reduction, nutritional supplements and just about everything else in here are meant to strengthen your immune system. Patients who pick up infections generally have weaker immune systems. When yours is strong, your body recognizes the germs and eliminates them. This is your best and most important strategy. The vitamins recommended in Chapter 9 are a vital element. Combine a good vitamin program with the stress reduction techniques you can choose from every chapter after this one and you will be much more resistant to infection than otherwise.

—Use certain Aromatherapy essential oils known to be hostile to bacteria and viruses that might be floating around. The details are in Chapter 13.

—If you are likely to have a urinary catheter, talk to your doctor about when to remove or change it. Urinary tract infections from catheters are the number one hospital infection. Many catheters are left in too long or changed inappropriately. An excellent article from *Consumer Action* describes the work of Dr. Saint at the University of Michigan Medical School to reduce urinary tract infections: Dr. Saint, head of the patient safety program recommends "that you ask your doctor if it's absolutely necessary that you have a catheter. If the answer is yes, ask when it can be taken out. Many hospitals will simply change catheters to prevent infection. But Saint says available data don't support this practice. Instead, he recommends that you request an antiseptic-coated intravascular catheter at all times. And if you will be needing a urinary catheter for more than two days, ask for one made of silver alloy."[4]

Antibiotics are not your best answer, either. Hospitals with the highest rates of hospital-acquired infections also have the highest rates of antibiotic use.[5]

What You Can Do to Avoid Medication Errors

It is possible for medication errors to occur in hospitals, although they are not so frequent as you might think. You have much more reason to be concerned about infection or a reaction to a correctly prescribed drug. All the same, I want you to get the idea that errors don't have to happen to you. There are a number of things you can do to prevent them. Think of yourself as both lucky and vigilant. Unnecessary drugs, wrong drugs, and drugs that conflict with each other all weaken your immune system. It is in your interest to keep your intake of medications as low as possible, with your doctor's agreement. Here are some strategies to minimize the possibility.

—Have a relationship with your doctors and nurses. Make sure they know what your concerns are. Show them you care about them and the difficulties they face while doing their difficult jobs. Be friendly with the nurses and ask for their help. The more they see you as a real person, the more attention you'll get. Ask about ways to minimize medications.

—Make a list of the medications you now take, plus any others your doctors have prescribed. Make sure it is legible. Bring it with you to all appointments. This list will be helpful to your surgeon and anesthesiologist and will bring you a greater measure of safety. This point is vital to your safety and bears repeating.

—Get a list from your surgeon of all medications you are supposed to have after surgery. Tape a copy to yourself before surgery (no safety or straight pins). Have a friend bring one with your hospital kit. Back in your room, make sure you are getting exactly what's on the list. Check the dosages. A decimal point can be misread. Have a support person there to check all medications you are being given. Ask what the name of the medication is and what it is for.

—Use the practices in the rest of the book that have been shown in studies to reduce need for medication and improve immune function.

—Do not insist on antibiotics (trying to make the doctor "do something") unless the doctor requires them as a medical necessity. Too many times, patients make it hard for the docs to say no, sometimes threatening them. Everybody wants to feel that something is being done for them, but I urge you to allow the doctors to do what they believe is needed, and no more.

—Since you will have unfamiliar and overworked nurses and staff giving you your medications, make sure they check your hospital ID bracelet, or already know who you are, before giving you anything. This is an extra safety check to ensure the medication you receive is meant only for you, and not for another patient.. Be friendly while asking for what you need. And, check this note from *Consumer Action*.

"Be particularly vigilant about medicines with similar names. The FDA even posts a list on its Web site of medications that are commonly confused, and it unfortunately isn't all that unusual for a nurse or pharmacist to grab the wrong bottle. For example, there are numerous reports of mix-ups involving Celebrex, an arthritis drug; Cerebyx, a seizure medication; and Celexa, an antidepressant."6

Here's some extra emphasis on the value of questioning the need for an antibiotic. Many patients develop a "hospital cough," or mild upper respiratory tract or bronchial infection. The authors of a study published in the Journal of the AMA say plainly: "although antibiotics have been shown to be largely ineffective in treating colds, upper respiratory tract infections and bronchitis, they are nevertheless prescribed to 51%-66% of patients diagnosed with these conditions." An estimated 12 million antibiotic prescriptions, or one fifth of all antibiotics prescriptions filled during 1992, were written for patients with colds, upper respiratory tract infections or bronchitis, "despite lack of evidence of their effectiveness in the management of these ailments. More than 90% of upper respiratory infections, including bronchitis and colds, are caused by a virus and are therefore impervious to antibiotics."7 The practice of dosing patients with antibiotics has contributed to the spread of antibiotic-resistant bacteria and consequent infections in community settings. The largest cause is patient demand. Ask yourself if you really want to insist on antibiotics for conditions they do not help, while at the same time they reduce your body's natural defenses. Such medications are useful when you are assured that the use has true medical value. Patients who try to pressure their doctors to give them antibiotics put the doctor in a difficult position.

A more recent study confirms an increase in antibiotic abuse. In 1980, an estimated 59% of patients who went to their doctors with a complaint of cough received an antibiotic prescription, as compared to 70% of patients who presented with cough in 1994. The increasing trend of antibiotic prescribing for patients with cough is, again, in the face of "increasing evidence of the lack of efficacy of antibiotic treatment in this condition."8

Medication Errors and Infection When Children Are the Patients

Children undergoing surgery are more at risk than adults and therefore need even greater protection and support. Ten percent of pediatric residents in one study made a 10-fold dosage error or greater, and 13.7% of all children admitted to hospitals have an Adverse Drug Reaction. Dosage errors are 93.7% of total drug mistakes. These errors are likely to be more serious in children.9 Another study of 1669 hospitalized children shows 45.7% of them had what are called "adverse clinical events," a category which includes all the bad things that can happen. Approximately 17% were adverse drug reactions.10

You can help your child by being present and alert, while maintaining a calm attitude. A confident and balanced state of mind is a good thing to hold for your child. You might also carefully check medications being administered to be sure they are on the list you got from the surgeon and that the dosages are the right amounts. Being friendly with the nurses helps your child.

Overprescription of antibiotics has, as you might expect, bigger consequences for children. A *JAMA (Journal of the American Medical Association)* report tells us that 44% of children with common cold, 46% of those with upper respiratory tract infections, and 75% of those with bronchitis received an antibiotic prescription, despite the fact that, as emphasized in the article, antibiotic treatment is typically ineffective in these conditions. These data indicate that 21% of all antibiotic prescriptions written for children younger than 18 in 1992 (over 11 million prescriptions) are unnecessary.11 Once again, I urge you to let the doctors do their jobs. Do not insist on antibiotics where they are not medically necessary.

Anesthesia for Children

Research at Yale University shows that children who cry and struggle as they're being given anesthesia suffer nightmares and heal more slowly than calm youngsters. About 65 percent of children experience high anxiety before an operation, especially those four or younger, who can't understand what's happening. Most of the anxiety occurs when children are taken away from their parents to undergo the anesthesia. The smell of the gas and the mask over nose and mouth are frightening, so the majority of young children cry and struggle to get away. In the study, approximately 40 percent of children undergoing outpatient surgery developed nightmares, separation anxiety or temper tantrums for weeks afterward. The more traumatic the anesthesia experience, the more problems followed.12

Many doctors aren't aware there is a problem, but the research showed that children who were calm before having their tonsils removed needed much less pain medication and returned to school sooner than upset kids. The best way to help a child through this experience is for the adults to stabilize their own moods, remaining calm, loving and supportive. It is very good for a calm mother or father to be hugging her or his child as the anesthesia is administered. Unfortunately, 30 percent of hospitals ban parents from being present. Try anyway. Tell the doctor about the Yale study.

On the other side of the coin, the worst thing a parent can do is get tense and ridicule the child by saying something like "tough guys don't cry," which almost always increases the crying and fear. Parents will help their child most by doing the practices in this book as if *they* were having the surgery. The parents' state of mind influences the child more than any other factor. This holds true even into the teens. In order to be calm yourself, for the benefit of your child, you need to practice, at least, the breathing and relaxation exercises in Chapter 5 and the imagery in Chapter 7. Use hypnosis or other techniques for increasing calm and reducing fear.

Whether a parent can be in the operating room or not, it is imperative to have a meeting with the anesthesiologist that includes your child. If you all get along, and the doctor sees that you will be a good influence and help things go better, you might be able to stay with your child through the anesthesia. Ask. If your child has developed even a moderate trust for the doctor during the meeting, it helps. This kind of preoperative support—meeting the doctors and getting comfortable, having the operation explained, and getting more familiar with the process—is very helpful.13

If you are unable to ease the tension from the situation naturally, some hospitals offer children a liquid sedative. It leaves youngsters relaxed and causes temporary amnesia, so those who still cry don't remember it, although they may retain partially buried traumatic memory. The medical industry considers it safe, but doctors must remember to give it 20 minutes before it is time for the anesthesia. As a parent, you have to balance the possible harm of nightmares and adverse behavior changes against your concerns about pharmaceuticals. Ask the anesthesiologist about the issue. While I recommend that your child meet him or her and, hopefully, find a feeling of relative safety, I also suggest that you have a separate conversation with the doctor (apart from your child, I mean) about potential anxieties. You can find a helpful anesthesia brochure, written for parents, online. See *Resources* for a link.

What Can You Do for Children?
Do the same as with adults, with the addition of a well-prepared parent. The parents ought to prepare almost as if they are having the surgery by reading the whole book and using the strategies to lower their own stress levels. The parents' state of mind influences the child's, even well into the teens, more so with younger children. Your peace of mind passes to your child, as does your stress.

A responsible, loving adult needs to be with a child in hospital all the time, if possible. The adult should have a list of prescribed medications with correct doses, clearly typed, from the supervising doctor. You need to check everything. Is it the right medication? Is the dose correct?

Older Patients
Numerous studies of medication problems with older patients show that seniors often have weakened immune systems, which makes for greater vulnerability. Three studies show that between 11% and 17% of older patients had Adverse Drug Reactions, preventable in about half the cases, the authors estimate. And 27% of older patients were, on admission to hospital, receiving unnecessary medications, while 12% were getting drugs with absolute contraindications.14

What Can You Do?
Take all the measure outlined above for adults and children. Older people often need more support to get through the process. Older patients may be at a level of risk similar to children, depending on the strength of their healing systems. Use more than one of the strategies for enhancing immune strength that you will find in almost every chapter.

Immune strength is by far your most important job. Also, medication dosage errors can be more significant than in a healthy 30 or 40-year old. You might want to refer back to Chapter 2, "Your Personal Support Team," for suggestions.

Medical Errors and What to Do to Avoid Them

As in every profession where people are working hard and under pressure, mistakes can happen. Our job as patients is to take care of ourselves and expect a good course of treatment. Most likely, that's what will happen. The best defenses are:

—Your balanced state of mind and the strength of your own healing system. You can help yourself quite a bit.

—Your friendly communication and connection with your doctors and staff, as discussed in Chapter 1.

—Your personal Support Team in the hospital with you, monitoring what you are given and helping your mood.

A Reassuring Note on Wrong-Site Surgery

Between 1996 and 2003, the Joint Commission on Accreditation of Healthcare Organizations has received about 150 reports of surgeries being performed on the wrong limb or organ, or even the wrong person. That's fewer than 25 a year in the US. From casual conversation, one might get the impression there are more. In fact, they are rare, but still remotely possible. US hospitals have this hazard pretty well handled. If there's any question, make sure you and your surgeon agree on what's happening before you enter the operating room. The Commission also recommends that you talk with your surgeon about what steps are being taken to identify the correct site for the procedure. For knee surgery, for example, you and the doc together mark the surgery knee with a "Yes" and the healthy one with a "No" using an indelible surgical pen. A simple "x" could mean yes or no.15

CHAPTER 4
Cultivating a Healing Point of View

"Through my research, I became convinced that beliefs have physical repercussions…that the human spirit is relevant, indeed influential, in the treatment and prevention of illness. In my thirty years of practicing medicine, I've found no healing force more impressive or more universally accessible than the power of the individual to care for and cure him—or herself."
Herbert Benson, MD, *Timeless Healing*

"The great majority of us are required to live a life of constant, systematic duplicity. Your health is bound to be affected if, day after day, you say the opposite of what you feel, if you grovel before what you dislike and rejoice at what brings you nothing but misfortune. Our nervous system isn't just a fiction, it's part of our physical body, and our soul exists in space and is inside us, like teeth in our mouth. It can't be forever violated with impunity."
Boris Pasternak, *Doctor Zhivago*

When you get something you don't want, such as surgery or illness, it brings an opportunity to focus more on what you do want. Some people actually make use of the opportunity by stopping, reflecting, and re-evaluating. I'm guessing that you are one of those, since you are here, looking to make your contact with modern medicine as good as possible.

What is your responsibility in the healing process? It begins with realizing that your body, mind, and spirit are fully involved in the situation. You are the one being healed, you are the healer and you are the healing. Let me encourage you to maintain this wisdom even though you may feel that the medical system might like you to be little more than a passive lump.

I know you want to participate in your surgical process. I think you know it is both possible and worthwhile to improve the entire experience, right up to and including your much-better-than-expected healing. While surgeons are doing incredible work these days with high skill, the healing part remains yours. All healing is self-healing, really. We are practicing self-healing when we visit a doctor, when we ask around for more knowledge about what we can do, when we ask for help and are open enough to receive it.

> "It's supposed to be a secret, but I'll tell you anyway. We doctors do nothing. We only help and encourage the doctor within."
> Albert Schweitzer, MD

Let's look at what our doctors actually do. Some good things, such as diagnosis and curing. Western medicine has excellent diagnostic tools. Docs usually do a great job of figuring out what's going on. Curing is what doctors do when things go right. Think of "curing" as one person giving another a treatment or medicine that alleviates the symptoms more or less completely. Much of our standard medical treatment comes from the belief that the doctor cures the patient. Sometimes that turns out to be true, as when an antibiotic saves your life from pneumonia or an action or procedure that makes the symptoms disappear completely. I feel deep gratitude to the researchers and doctors who have worked on these miracles. I deeply appreciate having my eyesight saved from a detached retina by a modern procedure in an eye center with all the latest equipment. The patient's traditional role is to receive the cure and obey the doctor. Many people like this way of doing business and prefer to be passive.

But passivity causes us to miss some of the possibilities of more complete healing, or perhaps just a more satisfying experience of wellness. What if it's closer to truth to say that the surgeon removes the obstacles in the way of the body healing itself? Self-healing is a function the human body has always performed and has always been intended to perform. Curing is not the same as healing, for the latter requires real activity from the patient. A commentary by Max Heindel, an early 20th century Rosicrucian, on the healings of Jesus makes this point well:

> "A "cure" is a physical process. Healing is radically different; there the sufferer is always required to cooperate both spiritually and physically with the healer...In every case where Christ healed anyone, this person had to do something; he had to cooperate actively with the great Healer before his cure could be accomplished. He said, "Stretch forth thy hand," and when the man did so the hand was healed; to another, "Take up thy bed and walk," and when he did so the malady disappeared; to the blind, "Go and bathe in the pool of Siloam," to the leper, "Show thyself to the priest, offer your gifts," etc. In every case there was active cooperation upon the part of the one to be healed, which helped the Healer. They were simple requirements, but they had to be complied with, so that the spirit of obedience could aid the Healer's work...Obedience, no matter whether that involves washing in the Jordan or stretching forth a hand, shows a change of mind, and the man is therefore in a position to receive the healing balm."[1]

The standard medical model is oriented to reacting to symptoms. I had a vivid experience of the difference a few years ago when a mysterious and maddeningly itchy rash broke out on my arms and began to cover my whole body. I tried home remedies, got some relief, but nothing really worked. Next, I wanted to know if the clinic MD knew what it was and what to do. He told me some things it wasn't, which was sort of reassuring, but he didn't know what it was. He gave me cortisone cream, a remedy good at suppressing symptoms but with no possibility of affecting the underlying cause, which he admitted he didn't know. Whatever internal process was disturbing my body would still be going on under the surface. The cause would not be dealt with and the symptoms would probably pop up somewhere else.

A friend sent me to an experienced traditional Chinese herbalist, who took my pulses (yes, multiple pulses), looked at my tongue, asked a few questions, and told me I had imbalance of wind, heat, and dampness in various organs. I needed coolness here, dry there, less wind, and this could be done with little round brown pills, which I took for four weeks. He also recommended avoiding foods that produce, as they say in Chinese Medicine, too much heat. I did what he said and it worked. Within 3 days, the symptoms decreased and were mostly gone in another week. I got an internal balancing and healing as well as a disappearance of symptoms. Not only did I get a diagnosis and treatment of the internal imbalance, I got to open a window into the great world of Chinese Medicine, practiced for 4000 years or so. Now, I'd seek the help of a practitioner of Chinese herbs or acupuncture for anything in the realm of medical mystery, for conditions suppressed, but not really healed, by standard medicine. Self-healing sometimes means being open to a suggestion of where to look for help.

"Every situation, properly perceived, becomes an opportunity to heal."
A Course In Miracles

Healing has always been fundamentally about becoming whole. We have bodies, you might say, other than the physical. I know we're conditioned to think of our bodies as sort of standing alone, but suppose it's not so. Suppose we have emotional, mental, and spiritual "bodies" as well. Why not? What if healing happens at a deeper level when these bodies are in tune with each other? Could a healing from a traumatic accident, for example, be complete when nightmares haunt you, dizziness walks with you, and your thinking isn't what it was, even though your body is repaired? The doctors pronounced you "cured" and told you there's nothing more they can do. The dizziness may exist in a part of your being medicine doesn't acknowledge. Healing yourself implies giving attention and respect to the parts of our beings that are not physical. That's what is meant by the term "Integrative Medicine."

A Healing Attitude

"Health is a state of complete physical, mental and social well-being, and not merely the absence of disease or infirmity."
Constitution of the World Health Organization

The second big item is to develop a healing attitude. What is that? It starts with a way of looking at your situation that is moving in the direction of both acceptance of the situation and responsibility for using all your resources and powers to heal yourself. A healing attitude includes willingness to expand your beliefs about your resources and powers to include more possibilities than you used to know. After all, how would you know what the limitations of your powers are if you, like most of us humans, use only a small part?

Lawrence LeShan, MD, who has researched the mind-body relationship for many years, suggests a powerful clue about what makes some people do well in treatment. Those who recover best from life-threatening cancer, he has found, have in common one thing. As he says it, they all "want to live their own lives and sing the songs of their own personalities." Neither fear of dying nor desire to live to serve the needs of others is enough to mobilize the healing powers within us. "When individuals," Dr. LeShan says, "understand this and begin to search for and fight for their own special music in ways of being, relating, working, creating, they tend to respond much more positively."[2] His insight applies to all efforts at self-healing.

One way to begin: adopt one attitude shift and go to some effort to be optimistic. If you are there, great. If you're not, the material here in the book can help, provided you are willing to play along a little. It's worth it. Optimists recover better. Norman Cousins, talking about the value of personal attitude in his book, *Head First, The Biology of Hope*, describes his stay in a sanitarium as a ten-year-old, after he contracted tuberculosis, at that time the major cause of death in children:

"The young optimists at the sanatorium didn't argue with the basic facts. They knew, however, that some kids did come through the ordeal. So long as this evidence was real, it fed their hopes and bolstered their will to live. Nothing to me was more striking than the fact that far more optimists were able to conquer their illness than were the realists."[3]

You don't have to be a Pollyanna to be optimistic, or smile when you don't feel like it. But ask yourself this: do the words that you most often speak reflect your real, chosen, response to the question: "What do you want?" Do you prefer possibilities to explore and entertain, or closed doors and dead-end paths?

> "A pessimist sees the difficulty in every opportunity; an optimist sees the opportunity in every difficulty."
> Winston Churchill (1874-1965)

Psychologists at UCLA studied whether optimism in the context of a stressor affected mood and immune changes in a group of law students. While there were no immune differences between optimists and pessimists at the beginning, those subjects who began the semester optimistic had more helper T cells and higher natural killer cell cytotoxicity mid-semester than subjects who had tested as pessimistic. Helper T cells are the "conductors" of the immune system, directing and amplifying immune responses. Natural killer cell cytotoxicity reflects the ability of these immune cells to kill cancer cells in the laboratory. Natural killer cells are thought to be important in immunity against viral infection and some types of cancers. The changes in the immune system are attributable to two psychological characteristics of optimists: they experience events as less stressful, and they show less negative mood, such as anxiety and depression. Researchers previously found that optimism about health outcomes among HIV patients has been associated with slower immune decline and later symptom onset.4

Even better, you need not even be realistic about your state of wellness. "Being overly optimistic may actually be healthy," says Dr. Geoffrey Reed of UCLA. "Our data," he wrote, "show that people who have a life-threatening illness can say these unrealistic positive things about their future and still behaviorally do things to take care of their health."5

Once you choose optimism, you are in a position to take in new ideas and take some control of your process. Allow yourself to feel grateful and lucky to be in a modern hospital, taken care of by friendly, well-educated personnel. The luckier you feel, the more good luck you attract.

Looking at pessimism for a moment, recent studies demonstrate that patients whose religious beliefs encouraged them to think that God was punishing, or abandoning, them, or that the devil caused their illnesses or that they were abandoned by their church, were more likely to die from their illnesses. Call it a strong form of pessimism, but it's also a profound misunderstanding, perhaps even an illness of mind and spirit. On the other hand, the same article, in *Christianity Today*, reports that "only 7 percent of the studies reported religious commitment had a negative effect on patients' health. Three quarters of the studies, conducted over the past two decades, reported a positive influence."6

One of the main points of The Book of Job seems to be encouragement of the idea that illness and misfortune are not necessarily caused by personal wrongdoing. Job's wealth was gone, his children killed, his health a memory. His "friends" grilled him about what he must have done to deserve all this, assuming he must have offended God. The primitive belief, that God (or the gods, if you wish) punishes those who offend Him and rewards those who please Him, still reverberates in a lot of contemporary religious ideology. Some people actually believe, in the face of daily contrary evidence, that rich and healthy people are good, while the sick and poor are bad and "deserve" what they get. How rich is life when reduced to such a simplistic, life-denying formula? It is true, though, that blaming yourself for getting sick or injured is linked to poorer health outcomes.7 Thinking "It's all my fault" is the essence of pessimism. Being wracked with guilt and self-blame is indeed hard on the immune system.

From another perspective, though, illness often appears to have a correlation to personality and behavior. It doesn't usually just come out of nowhere. Since guilt doesn't help, the most satisfactory viewpoint is probably that we are not to blame, but that we do better when we allow ourselves to be responsible to ourselves and to our physical condition. It is futile, though, to equate spirituality with good health, as Larry Dossey, MD points out:

> "There are people who break every commonsense rule of health and never get sick. They go to bed drunk every night, smoke four packs of cigarettes a day, live to be 100, and they're physically healthy to boot. I bet everyone knows somebody like that. Flip that over, though, and what you get are the unhealthy saints and mystics. These are the God-realized Olympic-class spiritual achievers, leading irreproachable spiritual lives. They do everything right spiritually, yet frequently their health histories are miserable...
>
> Is there a correlation between your thoughts, emotions and attitudes and your level of physical health?...The correlations are there, they're strong, and we would be foolish to ignore them. But are they invariable? No. Profound spiritual achievement

is no guarantee of physical health…It is possible to be highly spiritually realized and yet get awfully sick…

It may outrage our sense of cosmic justice, but spiritual achievement and physical health do not always go hand-in-hand. Sometimes the wisdom of the world works the other way, and the saints and sages suffer more than the wicked. Therein lies a paradox—and a mystery beyond our powers of scrutiny. And it is important to recognize this because otherwise it becomes all too easy to fall prey to the trap of self-blame when illness strikes."8

(The excerpt first appeared in the article "Healing and Prayer, The Power of Paradox and Mystery" by Larry Dossey, printed in the IONS Review #28, pp. 22-25, Winter 1993, and is reprinted by permission of the author and the Institute of Noetic Sciences (website: www.noetic.org). Copyright © 1993 by IONS, all rights reserved.

Larry Dossey, MD, is a physician of internal medicine and author of nine books focusing on the role of consciousness and spirituality in health, including the New York Times bestseller Healing Words and, most recently, Healing Beyond the Body. His website: www.dosseydossey.com)

Dossey refers to a story in John 9 in which the disciples ask Jesus about a man who has been blind since birth. One of them asks a question loaded with negative assumption: "Who hath sinned, this man or his parents that he is born blind?" And Jesus said "No one has sinned that this man is born blind, but that the works of God should be made manifest through him." The reasons for illness or injury may sometimes dwell beyond conscious understanding. The toxic idea that the righteous are well and the sick are sinners should be dismissed from our minds and our culture.

Here's another angle to consider. Stage 4 cancer patients, in a study combining blood analysis with psychological profiling, showed three major "patient profiles:" *Resignation, Nondirected Struggle*, and *Purposeful Action*. In *Resignation*, the patients were not hopeful and the blood analysis showed a depressed immune function. About patients described as being in *Nondirected Struggle*, the report said: "These patients appeared dissatisfied and worried, struggling and anxious, but their conflict was without direction." The *Purposeful Action* group tested stronger for immune factors and evidenced belief in their own abilities to affect their situations. To emphasize this crucial point, I quote this succinct restatement by author Jeanne Achterberg:

"The overriding conclusion was that, within the sample studied, there were three differing psychological profiles that appeared to represent a continuum, starting from an attitude of giving up, extending to an attitude of ambivalent struggle, and finally reaching to include a purposeful and positive striving to overcome the disease. These were related to distinct hematological profiles. Only in the most positive profile was the immune system seen to be enhanced."[9]

Further analysis showed that the most predictive factor in patient wellness was the patients' imagery. The researchers "found that the imagery was a singularly powerful and independent factor, and that it tapped something that was untouched by other psychological tests."[10] Summing up, Achterberg writes: "As for the immune system, the imagination has consistently proved to have the most directive influence. It has, as is said in the words of researchers, 'contributed the most to the variance.'" Chapter 7 contains interesting and specific instructions for healing imagery.

Perhaps you can allow your imagination to extend these findings to your own situation, no matter how small or major your illness or injury might be. The message to take away is that you can exert a strong positive effect on your own healing system. The rest of this book shows you how to use imagination, relaxation and other tools to get you into a frame of mind likely to help you do well. If you're not there now, don't despair. You will be able to use some of the clues I offer to change it for the better. Having a definite purpose, with respect to your illness and to your whole life, is good for your health.

Belief and Placebo

Allowing yourself to believe in your recovery is the next part of the healing attitude. Belief is the most powerful healing agent in the world. Dr. Herbert Benson cites, in *Timeless Healing*, numerous studies of heart patients showing a fantastic 70-90% healing rate with a placebo, where both the doctor and the patient expressed strong belief in the treatment. Many old placebo treatments for asthma, herpes, or ulcers, among others, worked well for years, but stopped working when the caregivers no longer believed in them.11

So-called placebo healings ought to be held in deep respect, since these are healings that happen when the patient has been given pills or treatment that are not "supposed" to do anything at all. Yet there is a persistent rate of placebo healing in double blind studies. The important thing about the placebo effect is that it is a true mind-body interaction in which genuine self-healing occurs, the real thing, the occurrence we all hope for. Dr. Benson believes it's so important and wonderful that it deserves a new name: he calls it *remembered wellness*. In other words, the body's memory of states of wellness can be triggered by the mind. This wonderful concept can be extended to shed light on the remarkable success experienced by hypnotists who help clients regress to previous states of wholeness. The client can return to present time with a detailed inner image of themselves at the peak of their health and vitality.

The balance of this book is about how to bring about this healing response to help you get better faster and more completely. To reinforce the point, let me recall to your attention what Jesus said about the healings that he performed. I'm citing Jesus because these stories are good examples, familiar to many. You don't have to be Christian to see the point.

"And, behold, a woman, who was diseased with an issue of blood twelve years, came behind him, and touched the hem of his garment: For she said within herself, if I may but touch his garment, I shall be whole. But Jesus turned him about, and when he saw her, he said, 'Daughter, be of good comfort; thy faith has made thee whole.' And the woman was made whole from that hour." (Matthew 9:20-22)

In another encounter, Jesus said to the centurion who believed that Jesus could heal his daughter without going to see her: "Go thy way, and as thou hast believed, so be it done unto thee." (Matthew 8:13)

Here is another expression of this essential idea Jesus wanted the disciples to grasp: "And when he was come into the house, the blind men came to him, and Jesus saith unto them, 'Believe ye that I am able to do this?' They said unto him, Yea, Lord. Then touched he their eyes, saying, 'According to your faith, be it unto you.' And their eyes were opened." (Matthew 9:28-30)

When Jesus cured an epileptic child after the disciples had tried and accomplished nothing, he told them why they had failed: "Because of your unbelief: for verily I say unto you, if ye have faith as a grain of mustard seed, ye shall say unto this mountain, Remove hence to yonder place, and it shall remove, and nothing shall be impossible to you." (Matthew 17:14-20) The healers, as well as the patients, must believe in the process. Are you and your Support Team optimistic enough to accept that nothing is impossible to you?

Your Immune System

Most of the suggestions and practices in this book are intended to build up your personal healing system. It is the most important contribution you can make to your recovery and subsequent wellness. It is the foundation of recovery and health. Immune system strength helps you heal faster from surgery or illness, helps you avoid hospital infections, and helps you overcome many types of adversity. Your whole being is under stress in the hospital: you have concerns about what's going to happen, little or no control, and infections trying to get you to be the host of their new party. Your immune system is under assault from the moment you enter. You receive a high return on your efforts to build your vitality before you go.

The oldest healing methods in the world are traditional shamanic practices. They are invariably directed at strengthening the mind, spirit and body of the patient, not so much at the outer causes of an illness. Getting sick is perceived as a letting down of the patient's personal shield, the personal vitality, which opens an entry portal for the disease agents. "Healing, for the shaman is a spiritual affair. Disease is considered to have origins in, and gains its meaning from, the spirit world," writes Jeanne Achterberg.[12] This view, long ridiculed by Western doctors and anthropologists as "primitive," is now finding its place with us. It seems a patient will do better by strengthening personal power, energy or vitality, whatever you want to call it. Greater vitality translates into a stronger immune system. That's what this book is mostly about. The doctors have the external agents of illness covered. That is their territory.

The nature of the immune system is to be in tune with your nervous system. That's why stress is now thought to be the trigger, and perhaps the root cause, of so many illnesses. Stress has a depressive effect on immune function. But because stress is a result of our response to events and conditions, a result of the thoughts and images that we entertain most frequently, we can do something about it. Deepak Chopra explains the internal connections exquisitely:

> "Nature is a thinking organism, and our own thinking is just one reflection of nature's thinking. Thoughts transform themselves into molecules, and these molecules, called neuropeptides (first discovered in the brain), are literally messengers from inner space. Therefore, to think is to practice brain chemistry and body chemistry because these receptors are not only on the neurons in the brain, they are on all the cells of our body...If you look at T cells and B cells and lymphocytes you find they are constantly eavesdropping on your internal dialogue. Somebody inside you is constantly having a conversation with themselves. One thing about this person: He/she/it never shuts up. And the immune cells are listening. Not only are they listening, they are participating in that same conversation, because they make the same peptides the brain makes when it thinks. In fact, there are neurobiologists who say there is no difference between the immune system and the nervous system—the immune system is a circulating nervous system. It thinks, it has emotions, it has memory, it has the ability to make choices and to anticipate events.
>
> We are discovering that our body is actually the objective experience of consciousness, just as our mind is the subjective experience of consciousness. But they're both inseparably one. The body is a field of ideas. When you say, 'My heart is heavy with sadness', your heart is literally loaded with fat chemicals. When you say, 'I'm bursting with joy', your skin is loaded with endorphins, interleukins and interferons, which are powerful immunobody regulators and powerful anticancer drugs.
>
> You and I are neither the body nor the mind; we are the creator of both, which is pure consciousness. It's difficult sometimes to express this in words, yet this has been, in fact, the wisdom of almost every spiritual tradition in the world. In ancient Vedic wisdom, for example, there is an aphorism that says, 'I am not the mind, I am not the body. I come within myself to create body and mind. I experience myself

subjectively as the mind. I experience myself objectively as the body and the physical universe. But I am neither – I am beyond both.' The aphorism goes on to say: 'I am That, you are That. All this is That. That is all there is.'

Understanding that consciousness is the creator of mind and body, I think, is really necessary for us to survive and create a new reality. Not only is the body a field of ideas, but so is the physical universe we inhabit."13

(The excerpt first appeared in the article "Timeless Mind, Ageless Body" by Deepak Chopra, printed in IONS Review #28, pp. 16-21, Winter 1993 and is reprinted by permission of the author and the Institute of Noetic Sciences (website: www.noetic.org). Copyright © 1993 by IONS, all rights reserved. Dr. Chopra's website is: www.chopra.com)

Everything that follows is intended to make practical use of Deepak Chopra's great idea. How do we recognize our power as creators of mind and body? How do we use this information to do ourselves some good?

Surgery brings on stress added onto your regular daily dose, which was so beautifully described by Pasternak at the top of the chapter. At the hospital, you are out of your element, more helpless than usual, at the mercy of others, and you don't know how the story turns out. So stress is both a natural part of the process and an obstacle to healing. Easing part of it increases your chances of having a good outcome. Preparing for surgery mentally has been proven helpful in reducing stress, allowing the healing system to do its job.

An analysis of 191 studies with 8,600 patient documents showed people who prepared for surgery mentally and physically had less pain, needed less pain medication, lost less blood, had fewer complications, and left the hospital sooner than those who did not.14

Law of Attraction

A lovely way to think about how the mind-body connection works is the idea of Law of Attraction. Imagine for a moment that your thoughts, words, pictures, and actions create an energy field radiating from you and attracting into your life people and circumstances attuned to those thoughts, words, pictures and actions. Suppose any thought combined with emotion (positive or negative) radiates out from you and attracts conditions, events, thoughts, and people in harmony with it. What if? The underside of this coin might look a bit scary, but the upside looks great: suppose you really do have the power to change external conditions by changing what you think, say, feel and do. I emphasize that you are not to blame for illness and injury, but you *are* responsible for your thoughts. You are capable of choosing new thoughts, even a new story about yourself to believe in. If you are not entirely 100% satisfied with what's happening for you, it is within your power to look for and find other thoughts to think and express.15 Chapter 5 is a good place to get some ideas.

Caring For Yourself

I mentioned the very human tendency to think less of ourselves when life presents us with a physical problem. Another piece of the successful surgery puzzle comes into view when we look at how we hold, or think about, whatever is happening with us. Can you love yourself right where you are sitting now? I find the following words on the subject, from Stephen Levine, illuminating:

> "You and I, we're conditioned. We walk across a room, we stub our toe. What do we do with the pain in our toe? We're conditioned to send hatred into it. We're conditioned to try to exorcise it and, and we cut the pain off. In fact, even many meditative techniques for working with pain are to take your awareness, your attention, and put it elsewhere. Just when that throbbing toe is most calling out for mercy, for kindness, for embrace, for softness, it's least available. In some ways it's amazing that anybody heals, considering our conditioning to send hatred into our pain, which is the antithesis of healing.
>
> The way we respond to pain is the way we respond to life. When things aren't the way we want them to be, what do we do? Do we close down, or do we open up to get more of a sense of what's needed in the moment? Our conditioning is to close down—aversion, rejection, put it away, denial. Nothing heals. That is the very basis on which unfinished business

accumulates, putting it away—I'm right, they're wrong; no quality of forgiveness. Where can there be healing in that?

We suggest that people treat their illness as though it were their only child, with that same mercy and loving-kindness. If that was in your child's body, you'd caress it, you'd hold it, you would do all you could to make it well. But somehow when it's in our body we wall it off, we send hatred into it and anger into it. We treat ourselves with so little kindness, so little softness. And there are physical correlations to the difference between softening around an illness—blood flow, availability of the immune system, etcetera—and hardness. You know, if you've got a hard belly and your jaw is tight, and that hardness is around your eyes, it's very difficult for anything to get through…

When the mind sinks into the heart, and vice versa, there's healing. When we become one with ourselves, there's healing."16

Let's consider again what we mean by "health." I don't believe that "not having obvious symptoms of a named disease" fills the bill, but I bet it's the most widely accepted meaning. Suppose we try "a state of physical, mental and social well-being, not merely the absence of disease or infirmity." The World Health Organization likes it. Could it work for you?

One of the healing voices of our time, known as Abraham, invites us to be aware in detail of how we are feeling: "The way you feel is your indicator of whether you're letting it in. Letting what in? Letting in well-being. Letting in the clarity that is really you and letting in the abundance that is natural to you. Letting in your resilience, your physical stamina, and your flexibility. Letting in your ability to intuitively know your path. Letting in your sensitivity to your surroundings, your opportunities to expand, and your joy and appreciation. Letting yourself be who you really are. Letting in whatever you desire."17

The Value of No Resistance

Another piece of the healing attitude is not resisting your condition or situation. Resistance is a form of attachment to the thing we resist. It's

Br'er Rabbit stuck on the tar baby: he didn't want to be stuck, but the more he struggled with it, the more stuck he got. Resistance brings on striving, by which I mean a tense over-efforting that is itself an obstacle to what you really want. When you resist or deny something, you give up the possibility of control over it, because you've made yourself more dense and contracted. The more contracted, the less you can do. On the other hand, non-attachment doesn't mean giving up and going limp.

I'd like to ask you to play along with the idea that you are not just your physical body. Suppose you truly are also an energy field, full of thoughts, emotions, sensations, and reactions. Imagine, also, that "the kingdom of heaven is within you," and you grant yourself permission to dwell in the subtler realms of your being. From the point of view of your higher self, you are aware your body has something going on, you take care of what you need to do, but you're not in fear, shock, or a panic state. When you are in touch with higher self, you are operating here now, in present time, moving with the current rather than struggling against it. Your actions are therefore more effective. The kingdom of heaven within you has no need to resist or reject anything, although, as I said, a little optimistic denial can come in handy at the right time. Stay tuned for neat ways to become friendly with your personal healing attitude, in mind, body, and spirit. They are on their way to you.

> "Anything that really frightens you may contain a clue to enlightenment. It may indicate to you how deeply you are attached to structure, whether mental, physical, or social. Attachment and resistance are appearances with the same root: when you resist by pulling away your awareness, the emotion is one of fear, and the contraction is experienced as a pull like magnetism or gravity; that is, attachment. That is why we often fear to open our minds to more exalted spiritual beings. We think fear is a signal to withdraw, when in fact it is a sign we are already withdrawing too much."
>
> Thaddeus Golas, *The Lazy Man's Guide to Enlightenment*

Another Aspect of Healing

Some people help themselves heal spiritually by holding and acting upon an idea of service to others. For many people who are not in good health themselves, wounded healers we might say, helping others provides deep life meaning. In Bill Moyers' book, *Healing and the Mind,* he quotes a doctor describing a patient, seriously ill and in constant pain, who had been a longtime member of a stress reduction and self-healing program: "This wounded woman would go help other people and tell her story and be part of that healing process. Even as her body disintegrated, her emotions and who she was as a person just glowed. She became a magnificent person."[18] It might be a part of your self-healing to consider playing a role in the healing of someone or something, when you are able. You don't have to be perfect, or even healthy, to act as a healer. Even when you are flat on your back, you can offer good thoughts.

CHAPTER 5
Breathing and Relaxation

"Breath restores me to my exact self."
Song of Solomon

"One must not forget that recovery is brought about not by the physician, but by the sick man himself. He heals himself, by his own power, exactly as he walks by means of his own power, or eats, or thinks, breathes or sleeps."
Georg Groddeck (1866–1934), German psychoanalyst. *The Book of the It*

Why is learning the skill of relaxation so valuable? I'll give you one good reason right away. Here's what we are dealing with: "Researchers Learn How Stress Slows Wound Healing," proclaims the headline in *Science Daily*. I quoted some of this report in Chapter 2.

"Scientists investigating why wounds heal more slowly on patients who are stressed have found that psychological stress can increase the levels of some hormones in the blood. These hormones can slow the delivery of certain compounds—cytokines—to the site of the injury to start the healing process. But if the process is slowed at the beginning, the wound will take much longer to heal, posing potentially serious consequences to patients recovering from surgery. This finding, reported in a recent issue of the Archives of General Psychiatry, is the latest clue to how psychological stress causes physiologic changes within the body, many of which can weaken a person's health. 'There is a lot in the medical literature suggesting, if possible, that a patient should not be under stress before surgery,' explained Jan Kiecolt-Glaser, professor of psychiatry and psychology at Ohio State University. 'Stress, depression and anxiety prior to surgery have all been associated with poor surgical recovery…When levels of cortisol increase, it suppresses the immune response. It either reduces the number of neutrophils that rush to the wound site or it controls the concentration of the cytokines necessary for healing.'"[1]

In plain language, stress slows wound healing. A surgery incision qualifies as a wound. Now, the good news: relaxing in the right way speeds up wound healing. Since most surgery patients are stressed to some degree, it follows that most surgeons are unaware of the real potential of the human body to heal itself after surgery or injury. Since the standard operating norm is a state of chronic stress for doctors and patients, imagine what a huge breakthrough is possible. With less stress, healing rates could change significantly. Doesn't it seem reasonable to learn this relatively simple skill? It starts with giving some attention to your breath. This is a short chapter, but really valuable.

The Power of Breath

Breath remains the foundation of relaxation, and therefore the foundation, also, of stress management and self-healing. I have coached guided breathing sessions for well over a thousand people over the years. It's one of my favorite things to do. Why? Because almost anyone can learn to use breath consciously to bring vital energy into his or her system, and nothing else enables us to let go of toxic, stressful material and thought more efficiently. Breath is well understood as one of the body's chief methods of elimination of physical waste. Why not then see it as also eliminating emotional and metaphysical waste? Breath activates energy in your other bodies (emotional, mental, spiritual) as well. It's OK if you don't believe in your other bodies, but you might want to imagine that a kind of source energy rides with each breath. I have seen so many bothersome items improve in guided breathing sessions that I have no doubt that a strong and subtle power is at work.

The great majority of clients have come in both over-breathing and under-ventilated, with a shallow but too-rapid breath habit. To healers who understand breath, this indicates that all their cells are under constant stress from an imbalance of oxygen and carbon dioxide, and insufficient quantities of both in the system. This stress at the cellular level is just as real to your body as meeting a bear in the woods or being nervous at work. Just as breathing can make you better, lack of correct breath can slow down recovery. Poor breathing means that every organ, every fiber, every cell, is under chronic stress. I suggest that you have a friend watch you when you're sitting quietly at a time when you don't know you are being observed. Have them count the number of breaths per minute. If the count is more than eight per minute in a resting state, you need some breath coaching.

Good things happen in your body when you breathe more deeply and more slowly, exhaling in a calm manner that involves neither pushing nor withholding the outbreath. Dr. Joseph Mercola, at his informative web site, suggests good reasons to get your breathing going:

"When volume, rate and attention level are all altered, dramatic physiological, and even emotional, changes can occur…Patients who have learned and used breath practice as a part of their daily personal system of self-applied health enhancement respond more quickly to treatment, no matter what type of physician they are seeing. Individuals who are well are able to remain well, adapt to greater stress and have greater endurance when they keep breath practice in their daily self-care ritual."[2]

Breathing consciously sends suggestions throughout your body that you really want aliveness and vitality. Your breathing patterns say more about your desire to live and be well than any other indicator. You can use any of the breathing exercises in this chapter to experience and transmute anxiety, worry, or fear. When you practice awareness of breath, you open the way to reducing stress and to relaxing more deeply than perhaps ever before. You are also in a much-improved position to make your words, prayers and intentional imagery effective. You can breathe life force into them. In most of the ancient languages we know about, the word for spirit is the word for breath.

Here are three simple techniques you can choose from. Take it easy at first, unless you're already a good breather. You can choose to lie down or sit up. Please do not think that you have to do all of these. As with the rest of the book, choose what feels best. I do, however, recommend trying them all. They're all good.

Simple Diaphragm Breathing (2-8 minutes):
Breathe in through your nose, not such a big breath that you strain, but not too small either. Not too slow, not too fast. Natural and easy.

Place your tongue gently on the roof of your mouth. Let your breath out through your nose, allowing the outbreath to take longer than the inbreath. Take in enough air and you won't feel like pushing on the outbreath. Just let it go. Relax all the muscles that keep your breath from flowing easily out. Practice makes the breath flow more easily. If your nose is blocked, breathe through your mouth.

When the air comes in, your stomach should expand smoothly. Make a smooth transition from inbreath to outbreath without pausing or holding your breath. When the air goes out, your stomach moves toward your backbone. You may notice some jerkiness at first. It will become smoother with practice. It takes only a little to get good at it. The chest and shoulders move gently in response, but you should not try to breathe high up in your chest.

Start with ten breaths in a nice easy, medium-deep flow, no huge effort. Count them. In plus out count as one. Play with this 3-4 times a day for a couple of minutes at a time until you feel a comfortable expansion of your stomach with each inbreath and a comfortable release of breath, *without pushing*. This is good for everyone, beginner or advanced breather. Repeat the number to yourself as you breathe in and as you breathe out (one…one, two…two…etc.).

When you get comfortable, think these words to yourself with each inbreath: *"Breathing in…I am breathing in life."* With each outbreath, think to yourself, *"Breathing out…I am letting go."* As you do this, let yourself feel the truth of it. Notice the sense of well-being that comes to you. Even if your nose is blocked, try to inhale as much as you can through it before switching to mouth breathing. Observe each breath. Notice whether you hold your breath after you inhale or exhale. Gradually let go of the holding, so that your breath flows evenly, without pausing. Count the breaths and watch them calmly. Notice thoughts coming up. Observe them and let them go without getting wrapped up in them. Keep counting. Use, in your mind, a word like "later," or "noticing" for the thoughts that come to mind.

When I first started doing this, I could hardly count to ten before my mind got completely tangled up in what someone said to me, or something I'd done. I realized I couldn't help getting distracted. What a wake-up! On the whole, it works better to laugh about this rather than self-criticize. Notice how you feel. If you are light-headed, stop here. It simply means you are not used to breathing and your body has to adapt.

Nothing harmful is happening. It means you have at last found a way to give your cells what they need, but to which they are not accustomed. If you're OK so far, do two more rounds of ten breaths. Can you work your way up to five sets of ten breaths? Can you count to ten five times? It can be a challenge.

A Quick Exercise

Whenever you feel tension, or when you feel like responding quickly with anger, take a full breath and let it out smoothly before you say or do anything. This will improve your mood and your relations. This simple little practice can change your whole day, interrupt a downward spiral, and bring you into the present, where resides all the power that ever was or will be. Nervous? Annoyed? Angry? Breathe first. Consider. Then choose a somewhat better thought.

Think again and again about connecting your breaths to each other. When you come to the top of the breath, let go of all the muscles that might hold it in. Let go right at the top—no pausing. When your breath has let itself out, so to speak, inhale without a pause or break. Think of your breath as one continuous thread, unbroken by halts or pauses or holding, flowing in and out easily. Do 22 connected breaths, then relax. This is a powerful practice. To take it further, you need a coach trained in conscious breathing or Rebirthing as taught by Leonard Orr.

Alternate Nostril Breath (3-5 minutes).

This is so useful and wonderful there's no way to express it adequately. One of its many benefits is that it opens the way to a good night's sleep. It is a terrific stress reliever. Here's how you do it:

Take your index finger and middle finger of your right hand and place them on your third eye, about an inch up from where your eyebrows would meet. Your thumb rests on the right side of your nose, your third finger on the other. Exhale through both nostrils. Gently squeezing the right nostril with your thumb, breathe in through the left nostril only. Now hold your third finger over your left nostril while releasing your thumb and breathe out through your right. Then inhale through your right and breathe out through your left. Pause briefly after each exhalation. Count to four on the inhalation and eight counts for the exhalation. If eight is hard, six will do until you are comfortable. Do five to ten rounds.

For a deeper explanation of the purpose of this exercise and precise instructions, I'll quote from a wonderful book called *Nature Cure*, written around 1900, when America was enthusiastic about natural healing methods. It is precisely what I was taught 30 years ago by an Indian yogi. It may sound far-fetched to you, but I assure you it is well grounded in 4000 years of practice. You have to try this one to know how good it is.

"Rhythmical Breathing

The breath entering through the right nostril creates positive electro-magnetic currents, which pass down the right side of the spine, while the breath entering through the left nostril sends negative electro-magnetic currents down the left side of the spine. These currents are transmitted by way of the nerve centers or ganglia of the sympathetic nervous system, which is situated alongside the spinal column, to all parts of the body...

The balancing of the electro-magnetic energies in the system depends to a large extent upon this rhythmical breathing, hence the importance of deep, unobstructed, rhythmic exhalation and inhalation.

In order to establish the natural rhythm of the breath when it has been impaired through catarrhal affections, wrong habits of breathing, or other causes, the following exercise, practiced not less than three times a day (preferably in the morning upon arising, at noon, and at night), will prove very beneficial in promoting normal breathing and creating the right balance between the positive and the negative electro-magnetic energies in the organism.

The Alternate Breath

Let your breaths be as deep and long as possible, but avoid all strain...Alternate breathing may be practiced standing, sitting, or in the recumbent position. The spine should at all times be held straight and free, so that the flow of the electro-magnetic currents be not obstructed. If taken at night before going to sleep, the effect of this exercise will be to induce calm, restful sleep.

While practicing the "alternate breath," fix your attention and concentrate your power of will upon what you are trying to accomplish. As you inhale through the right nostril, will the magnetic currents to flow along the right side of the spine, and as you inhale through the left nostril, consciously direct the currents to the left side.

The more positive the demand, the greater the supply. Therefore, while breathing deeply and rhythmically in harmony with the universal breath, will to open yourself more fully to the inflow of the life force from the source of all life in the innermost parts of your being.

This intimate connection of the individual soul with the great reservoir of life must exist. Without it, life would be an impossibility."3

For most of us, one nostril is habitually more open than the other. If you breathe on a hand mirror (through your nose, of course), the patch of mist from one nostril will be larger than from the other. In a healthy person, this dominance naturally switches several times in a day. As a sort of early warning signal for coming illnesses, though, one nostril can become too dominant, which represents life energies out of balance. This exercise rebalances your life energies and brings about conditions for the restoration of health. Current neuroscience research confirms that the practice of alternate nostril breathing helps to balance the right and left hemispheres of the brain and your electrical polarities.4

Dr. Weil's Favorite Breathing Exercise

Dr. Andrew Weil has long been a student of healing breath and is worth listening to. He adds the following comments and another powerful breathing practice in response to a question:

"As the day of your surgery approaches, you may experience heightened anxiety. Relax. That's the most constructive piece of advice I can offer. Neutralizing stress can ease any symptoms or discomfort you feel and give your immune system a boost. The American Psychological Association published a study just last year that found preoperative patients who had been taught relaxation techniques not only had less anxiety but also left the hospital sooner and had fewer post-surgical complications. Practice my breathing exercise at least twice a day.

Here is a yogic breathing exercise I have long recommended to my patients as a means of stress reduction:

Sit up, with your back straight (eventually you'll be able to do this exercise in any position).

Place your tongue against the ridge of tissue just behind your upper front teeth and keep it there throughout the exercise.

Exhale completely through your mouth, making a whoosh sound.

Close your mouth and inhale quietly through your nose to a mental count of four.

Hold your breath for a count of seven.

Exhale completely through your mouth, making a whoosh sound to a count of eight.

Repeat this cycle three more times for a total of four breaths.

Try to do this breathing exercise at least twice a day. You can repeat the whole sequence as often as you wish, but don't do it more than four breaths at one time for the first month of practice. This exercise is fairly intense and has a profound effect on the nervous system—more is neither necessary nor better for you."[5]

The Relaxation Response

Moving into intentional relaxation is next. It's the logical next step after learning how to breathe, and because it has the great virtue of having been extensively studied and widely used in hospitals for over 28 years. There are a number of relatively simple techniques that people use. One widely-studied approach known as the Relaxation Response is a simple exercise that delivers more than it promises.

In 1975, Dr. Herbert Benson, of Harvard Medical School, published a book called, sensibly, *The Relaxation Response.* Dr. Benson explained how anyone could do this uncomplicated method to achieve increased inner peace. Not only does it help your state of mind; it also helps bring significant improvements in a wide array of medical situations, including improved recovery from surgery, as he and others have demonstrated in many clinical trials.

Here is a practice easily available to and compatible with just about everyone. There are lots of ways to relax, so if you have a practice you are happy with, keep doing it. This one is as straightforward as can be. It's a very useful and powerful tool, yet surprisingly simple. Before I give you the instructions, I want to impress you with how real a response you can get from your body. Here's a quick summary of the Relaxation Response studies cited by Dr. Benson:6

—Patients with hypertension experienced significant decreases in blood pressure and needed fewer or no medications over a three-year measurement period.

—Patients with chronic pain experienced less severity of pain, more activity, less anxiety, less depression, less anger, and they visited the managed care facility where they received care 36% less often in the two years after completing the program than they did prior to treatment.

—Seventy-five percent of patients with sleep-onset insomnia (meaning that they couldn't fall asleep easily) were cured and became normal sleepers. Sleeping also improved for the other 25%, and most patients took significantly fewer sleep medications.

—Patients with cardiac arrhythmias experienced fewer of them.

—Patients who had open-heart surgery had fewer post-operative arrhythmias and less anxiety following surgery.

—Patients with cancer and AIDS experienced decreased symptoms and better control of nausea and vomiting associated with chemotherapy.

—Patients undergoing painful X-ray procedures experienced less anxiety and pain and needed one-third the amount of pain and anxiety medications usually required.

What is there to lose by learning how to release stress? A good time is just after a brief warm-up with one of the breath practices. Here is a simple program you can easily do.. For information about the Relaxation Response, see Dr. Benson's books, *The Relaxation Response* and *Timeless Healing*.7

How to Do A Simple Relaxation

Pick a word or short phrase that you feel good about. It could be anything. It doesn't have to be spiritual. More about that in a moment.

—Sit quietly in a comfortable position.

—Close your eyes and relax your muscles

—Breathe slowly and naturally. Repeat your focus word, phrase, or prayer silently to yourself as you exhale.

—Quietly ignore everyday thoughts or chatter. When thoughts

arise, say a word or phrase ("Later" or "Noticing," or "Oh well.") and gently return to your repetition.

—Set a timer for 10 minutes your first time. Sit quietly for a minute after the timer sounds, allowing other thoughts to return. Then open your eyes and sit for another minute before getting up. You can lengthen this up to 20 minutes if you like, but you don't have to. Twice daily, or at least once. Add it to your daily routine, like washing your face.

How do you pick a word or phrase? If you are in a religious tradition, you have a wealth of possibilities. Here are a few to get you started finding your own. Choose one. You can always trade it in. I doesn't matter what it is as long as it feels good to you.

One…Peace…Ocean…King of Kings…Mother of Mercy, pray for me…Lord Jesus, have mercy on me…Shalom…Adonai…Baruch… Om…Om Namaha Shivaya…Muh!…Peace…Love…Unity…One… Holy…Allah…

Or you can listen quietly until your own seed sound comes to you.

Your daily practice now consists of one or two little sessions containing a breath exercise and the relaxation. I suggest starting right now. This chapter has laid the groundwork for what follows. In the next chapters, I show you how to build on this foundation. These are skills you easily learn and improve with practice.

CHAPTER 6
The Power of Words to Boost Your Healing System

"Remember that all things are only opinion and that it is in your power to think as you please."
Marcus Aurelius

"So shall my word be that goeth forth out of my mouth: it shall not return unto me void, but it shall accomplish that which I please, and it shall prosper in the thing whereto I sent it."
Isaiah 55:11

What if you lived in a world in which every word you spoke were a word of power? Everything you said would roll forth from you, a declaration of your vision and expectation, and return to you fulfilled. Would you be thrilled if you woke up in such a world? Or would you be worried because you know you sometimes say things you really don't want?

I would love you to suspend your disbelief willingly and play along just for a while. Pretend, a little, that our thoughts become our realities, a little fuzzily maybe, so the pattern defies detection. Imagine your thoughts and words attracting to you similar thoughts and words, even actions. Allow yourself to entertain the possibility that people, experiences, events, situations, and things are pulled toward you by your thoughts and words. Remember Law of Attraction? For this chapter, at least, I ask that you make believe your words make a difference in how you feel and in how fast and well you recover.

How do your words make you feel? I invite you now to bring to mind a time when you felt a strong thought of anger or worry. Say the word: "furious" out loud. Go ahead and remember someone or something you have been furious at. Now, notice the feel of your body's response. Angry thoughts and words stimulate adrenal gland activity, which sends adrenaline coursing around your bloodstream, which brings on other body changes and takes energy that would otherwise support your aliveness. If you can bear to recall being furious, you'll feel the changes in your stomach. To clear this feeling, say out loud: "Even though I feel this anger, I deeply completely accept myself."

Now bring to mind a time when you felt really good, an achievement you feel proud of, or a time when you felt loved. Say the key word: "love" or "I am happy and loving" or any phrase that feels exhilarating. Notice the physical response. The chemicals you send around your system now are much better for you. Want to strengthen your immune system immediately? Words, simple words you say to yourself, can do it. Read on.

The brilliant book, *Message From Water* contains dark field microscope photographs of water crystals under various controlled conditions. One picture sequence features distilled water in jars. The experimenters spoke or taped written words or phrases, one to a jar. Some jars received positive expressions such as "love" or "thank you" or "I appreciate you." Others got insult words such as "I hate you" or "you fool!" The water receiving love and appreciation formed beautiful structured hexagons. The water getting the insults turned chaotic, swirly, and deeply ugly. The prayer of a Shinto priest over polluted lake water produced the most beautiful crystal of all. Give yourself a big treat and see the pictures online at Dr. Emoto's web site, listed in *Resources*, or buy the book. I found it astonishing and encouraging. Seeing these incredible photos makes the power of words evident. The water crystals are indicators of how our energy bodies respond to thought. It just happens we can perceive these signs, while subtler energy reactions are also going on beyond our ability to measure. You and I are about 65% water by weight. What if you could alter the structure of the water in your body by means of the words you carry around with you? What if you could alter any subtle energy or structure in your body with thoughts and words?

Words come from, express, and reveal beliefs. And you might as well believe that your beliefs are powerful, even when you aren't sure what they are. Most of us don't really know what we believe, deep down, until we come up against a crisis, or unless we engage in consciously setting out to know ourselves more deeply, and that happens mostly when something hasn't worked out. Unfortunately, it's reasonably certain that not everything you believe is good for you or your health. Consider the following story from The Washington Post:

"Ten years ago, researchers stumbled onto a striking finding: women who believed that they were prone to heart disease were nearly four times as likely to die as women with similar risk factors who didn't hold such fatalistic views. The higher risk of death, in other words, had nothing to with the usual heart disease culprits—age, blood pressure, cholesterol, weight. Instead, it tracked closely with belief. Think sick, be sick.

"That study is a classic in the annals of research on the "nocebo" phenomenon, the evil twin of the placebo effect. While the placebo effect refers to health benefits produced by a treatment that should have no effect, patients experiencing the nocebo effect experience the opposite. They presume the worst, health-wise, and that's just what they get.

"'They're convinced that something is going to go wrong, and it's a self-fulfilling prophecy,' said Arthur Barsky, a psychiatrist at Boston's Brigham and Women's Hospital who published an article earlier this year in the Journal of the American Medical Association beseeching his peers to pay closer attention to the nocebo effect. 'From a clinical point of view, this is by no means peripheral or irrelevant.'"[1]

Way too many of us spend a lot of energy thinking about what we don't want, or dreaming of all the bad things that might happen to us, or just reflecting about some present grim reality. Suppose, for a moment, that it really is true that you and I, all of us, attract more of whatever we think about most? 'Well and good," you might say, "but I have to be realistic, don't I?" Yes, you do, if you want more of that version of reality.

Reality appears to have many different versions. If you declare yourself a "realist," is it true or honest to believe that there are no other realities possible than the one you presently believe in? How can it be "realistic" to cling to one version of reality (think of it as a "reality tunnel") while denying or ignoring other versions? For now, let's say that attention to some particular thing or thought pattern brings more of that something. Then the best question to ask is: "Does what you say to yourself and others express what you really want?" I recommend you do anything you can to get *off* the subject of what you do not want, and give effort and thought to getting *on* the subject of what you *do* want. Do you pay more attention to what you want than what you don't want? If not, why not start now?

A Short Practice of Great Value

Write at the top of a page in a notebook the words: "I DESIRE WITH ALL MY HEART:" It may seem corny to you, but give it a chance, OK? Write down your desired outcome from your surgery. What do you want physically? What activities do you want to do as well as before, or better? Emotionally – do you want to feel happier, more loving? Writing it down absolutely clarifies what you believe. It also can help form a clear idea of where you will arrive.

Describe your surgery/health goals in four ways. How do you want to feel:

—Physically?
—Emotionally?
—Mentally?
—Spiritually?

Try for one sentence each, but it's OK to do more until you've said what you want to say. The next piece of the game is to make one sentence that states the most important parts right now. When you've got one sentence, I recommend using the formula that follows:

"I will apply all my powers to achieve the following aim."

Then write and say your sentence. When you do this, you are bringing in powers you know about and powers you might not be aware of, such as the power of your subconscious mind to bring people, things, or experiences to you in amazing, even miraculous ways. Say the formula and your brief statement three times a day.

> "Half this game is ninety percent mental."
> Yogi Berra

The Fine Print

Now I'll reveal the inner secret. It goes to the heart of the matter of use of speech and, ultimately, effective prayer, as you'll see in the next chapter. Suppose you want health in one of your organs, let's call it your kundabuffer organ. You say to yourself, "Oh my aching kundabuffer" since it happens to be hurting: "Please bring me health in my aching kundabuffer," you call out. But what are you actually concentrating on? Are you truly focused on health, or more on the ache? Please take careful note of this important distinction. Get your head around this. It's easy to imagine (incorrectly) that you are concentrating on health when you are really thinking obsessively about your pain, illness, injury, or lack of health. What you really give attention to is likely to increase. Why not believe in a reality in which you can structure your use of words to change your thought patterns?

To make an effective statement, two things seem to be needed: first, you need to allow your reality model to include the notion of thoughts having effects. Second, you must make the hoped-for reality more vivid in your imagination than the present, even if the present seems like a fixed "grim reality." You can do it.

Internal Dialogue

All of us talk on and on to ourselves in our heads. One of the uses of meditation practice or the Relaxation Response is to help us notice the nature and frequency of our chattering mindstuff. A practice like this helps with a universal human problem: our descriptions of ourselves. Some of us get absorbed in guilt, shame, or depression around having any kind of health problem, as if we had failed somehow. You might even have come to believe that it's your fault. You might observe self-talk along these lines:

—This is my fault.
—I always do things badly.
—People won't like me if I ask for what I want.
—I've had a lot of health problems and I'm likely to have more.
—I'm going downhill.
—I'll never recover my strength.
—Something's wrong with me.
—I have bad luck.

Do you find yourself saying or thinking any of those things about yourself? If so, try this:

1. Stop. 2. Breathe. 3. Reflect. 4. Choose a new thought, one that serves you now.

One more bit of fine print: you might have the habit of speaking of your illness as "my (name of illness)." If you really don't want it, I suggest you not take personal possession of it. When you say "Oh my scrofulous kundabuffer," you are reaffirming your personal ownership of this bad condition that you do not want. Guess what? When you increase your ownership interest, the condition tends to increase and persist. It belongs to you, doesn't it? Try this little game: Notice when you are using the possessive pronoun in front of something you don't want. Think of the words "I" and "my" as sacred, to be used consciously about things you know you want. Think of it like this: the universe is cooperating with you by giving you what you say you desire, based on your signals.

Healing Yourself

A method I've used successfully with clients and in workshops is writing and saying (out loud) some well-chosen words. The main thing to know about words for healing is that they must feel right; they must feel believable to our inner selves. When strung together in sentences, I call them "healing response statements," We say a statement, then allow and watch for awareness of our inner response. Our inner response will tell us when a statement resonates. That's the healing response. In truth, whatever comes is a healing response, for it always points you back in the right direction. I've found they work well when I use them to stimulate and examine my mind's responses to them. For a trial run, try saying this phrase out loud, at the same time listening for and allowing your real reaction:

"I am at peace with myself."

Whatever reaction you hear or feel, note it down in a few words. Say the statement again and notice what you feel. Write down your mind's answer. You are not trying to convince yourself that this statement is true right now, but to use it to find out what thoughts, feelings, and/or body sensations, are lurking in you just below the surface. That's the stuff in the way of your accepting the reality of the healing statement. It's like fishing. Try it one more time and look for a sense impression that might flash into your brain. Write down what you get. However you react, whether visual, auditory, or body feeling, your natural response is right for you. Next, add your name to it: *"I, (your name), am at peace with myself."* You also get to consider the desired reality, to taste it, become more familiar with it.

Note your response. Then, in the second person, as if someone else were talking to you: *"You, (your name), are at peace with yourself."* This helps heal negatives said directly *to* you in the past. Finally, in the third person: *"(Your name) is at peace with himself."* Using the third person helps heal negative statements made *about* you, whether you overheard them or not. Listening to your inner response is the key element.

Here are some healing statements that many people have found heartening. As with the other material in the book, choose the ones you feel good with. Pick one at a time and write it 5 times in each person: I, you, he or she. Say it out loud, too. If you do this once, or even twice, a day, you'll find it's a powerful self-healing tool. Try saying them to the mirror, looking into your own eyes. Or just read them to yourself a few times and notice how you feel. Anything you can do to make these sorts of thoughts more familiar is good for you. Use them in support of the aim to which you have pledged to apply all your powers. Play with them if they feel good to you.

Healing Response Statements

—I have a heartfelt desire to be well; I see myself as active and filled with good energy

—I am one with the Creative Force within me that knows how to bring about my highest good. I allow it.

—I recognize that within me lives natural wisdom and natural protection, which allow me and my body to stay healthy and strong. I let them work.

—I have the right to heal my body well on our own schedule.

—The place in my body that is about to receive the repair is highly receptive to allowing this repair and healing to happen for my highest good.

—From the moment I decided to have surgery, my recovery process started. I allow the healing to occur.

—All of the systems of my body are assisting and cooperating with the procedure, helping create my healing.

—With every conscious breath I take, I grow in vitality and well-being.

—My cells are filled with aliveness.

—All the cells of my body are bathed and illuminated in the perfection of divine essence.

If you know someone you can team up with, try the following method: I especially recommend you start with the last two statements just above. I've seen them light people up wonderfully when done in pairs:

Sit down opposite each other. Breathe medium-deep, nice and even. Look into each other's eyes. Person A says the statement in its "I" form. Person B receives and breathes in the statements. Do this five times, then switch to the "You" form five times. Switch so that B speaks and A receives. Say them loud, soft, fast, slow, wherever the spirit leads you. Have fun. Take 5 turns each.

Then make one change: Person B responds simply: "I know." Nothing else. Do five rounds. Play with it: Say it slow and fast, say it loud and soft, say it any way you think of. There's no way I can tell you how great this exercise is until you experience what happens.

What Do You Hear When You Talk to Yourself?

Let's look at some of the don't-wants we dug up a while back. What do we do with the fears, doubts, and negatives when they come up for us? One reassuring thought is that nearly everyone is running similar tapes in their heads. Relatively few illumined beings are free of negativity, and even they can be pulled into it if they happen to catch a little TV. Accept it. Observe it happening. The Relaxation Response is useful for this. Next, from a relatively calm place, reach for a slightly better thought. What's that? Well, suppose you know you're having a discouraging or frightening thought. It makes you feel bad. Feeling bad makes you feel worse, as the temptation is ever-present to reach for a worse thought, which makes you feel even worse. So a better thought is one that makes you feel better, even slightly. There's no point in trying to come out of being anxious or fearful by reaching for high and unrealistic thoughts. Slightly better will do. Once you're OK with that, you can work up to an even better thought, and so on, step by step. There's no gain in indulging thoughts that make you feel bad. You can tell the difference: all you have to do is pay close attention to how you feel.

"These are the times that try men's souls" can be fairly said of any personal difficulty that sends us into ourselves. A surgery definitely qualifies. What matters most to our well-being is how we respond. Can we use the challenge to see ourselves differently? I know it may not look like it now, but I would be negligent if I did not tell you that many people bear witness that their illness or their accident was a blessing. Why? Because it caused them to ask themselves the big life questions like: Am I going in the direction I want in life? Is there anything I need and want to change? How can I get from where I am to fulfilling my purpose for being on earth? Do I need to make amends to anyone, anywhere? Could I be kinder?

For now, I suggest that you simply notice your thoughts and be gentle with yourself. You might consider writing out new healing statements to affirm just how you want things to be. Suppose, for example, I observe myself talking in my head to the effect that I'll never be strong and active again. This is not an uncommon idea for people to buy into. I have come across quite a few people over 45 who think that when they have tennis elbow for a couple of months, it's all downhill from here. I got way too involved in downward spiral thinking when I had a frozen shoulder for a year. Nothing I knew seemed to be working and the pain was intense. I thought I would never run and jump and play again. Depression set in, along with frustration, helplessness, and fear of unchecked decline. It was scary. Here's what the beings known as Abraham suggest we say to ourselves

"There are many people who are right now experiencing the dream that is coming for me, who were at one time standing right where I am standing. I'm right on track. Everything is unfolding perfectly right where I am and gravitating to something that will satisfy me even more."2

The first element is the dream. What do you really want? What thought or plan is exciting enough that you can hardly wait to get to it? Write it down. Second, accept where you are. Third, others have moved beyond the place you are in. Fourth, realize you are part of a flow that moves you for your highest good…when you allow. Fifth, the "even more" implies that there is also satisfaction in where you are standing right now. Without being OK with where you are standing now, you'd be stuck. It seems wisest to start by acknowledging what is good, acceptable, and lucky about the present circumstance.

Talking With Your Body

> "Your brain can learn how to change immune response."
> David Felten, MD, in Bill Moyers, *Healing and the Mind*

One of the most enlightened of all Americans, George Washington

Carver, said: "If you love it enough, anything will talk with you." He recognized the life force in everything, finding no place or thing where it did not dwell. If it lives in peanuts and soil and the whole plant kingdom, if it works through animals, why wouldn't it be true for your body? Or one part of your body? You can find something to practice this on any place, any time. If you're stuck in a hospital hallway on a gurney, waiting to go into surgery, look around for something to love. The ceiling? Your big toe? A person? Your liver? Have you ever really practiced loving everything in your environment as much as you'd practice piano or tennis or TV watching? Practice loving the part of you that is not well. Say nice things to it.

It is said that love conquers all, that perfect love drives away fear. I don't mean feeling "in love" or erotic fascination. I'm thinking of transpersonal, even impersonal, love, the sort that keeps the world functioning. Consider the following possible characterization of love: *It consists of tolerating the manifestations of other beings.* Think of it. Most of us don't have to leave our houses to find other beings whose manifestations we can hardly tolerate. Most assaults and murders happen within the family when one person can't tolerate another. Accomplishing this version of love is a bigger task than it might seem at first. Extend your toleration to include all the parts of yourself and all your manifestations, as well as those of other beings. What if it freed up some energy for you?

In Chapter 2, I suggested a mini-ritual to thank the body part being repaired, or perhaps removed, for serving you as it has. Allow yourself to come up with words of love and appreciation for your body, and those parts, at this time. There is no greater healing force.

Allowing.
You can do this in a few seconds anywhere at any time.
—Notice something going on. Send allowing to it.
—Notice something going on you don't like. Send allowing to it.
—Notice something you do like. Allow it in.

Having fun? Do some more when you feel like it—in the car, at work, at home. Try it for a few minutes in a public place. Life offers limitless opportunities to allow.

You may recall that the Lord's Prayer asks that we be forgiven our trespasses, or our debts, as we forgive our trespassers, or debtors.

The most overlooked single word in the Bible has got to be "as." The prayer asks that we be forgiven, allowed, tolerated, or loved, in the same measure and manner as we forgive, allow, tolerate, or love. Not more, not less. The same as. Those who use that prayer always receive what they ask for. Everyone does, really, but most of us don't pay close attention to what we ask for. What if you simply ask, intentionally, on purpose, in words, for what you really do want for yourself?

Segment Intending

Segment Intending is a great concept brought to us by the Abraham I have mentioned.3 Simply put, every time you begin an action you think of your intention for this little segment of life. When you get in your car, you might intend a safe and pleasant journey. Reverent Hawaiians greet the ocean with respect when they enter, both asking permission from the divine realm and intending safety and joy.

How can you use it? When you get up, intend a good day. When you make breakfast, intend a great breakfast. When you get in a car, intend a safe and worthwhile trip. When you see the doctor, intend a positive healing experience. When you go for an operation, intend a great outcome, intend that it will go really well. Intend to be happy for the next five minutes. This neat practice, if you play around with it for a while, helps your mind stay clear and in present time.

Healing Statements for Your Medical Team

In her wonderful book, *Prepare for Surgery, Heal Faster,* which I recommend highly, Peggy Huddleston suggests that you ask your surgeon and anesthesiologist to read prepared healing sentences to you during your procedure. This is a wonderful use of words and a brilliant idea that capitalizes on recent understanding of the heightened suggestibility of surgical patients. Only in the last few years have doctors realized that patients in the anesthetic state are, in effect, in hypnosis, and that anything said to them is acted upon by their subconscious minds. Huddleston has pioneered this idea in workshops, consultations and her book over the past 20 years.

Many studies, in addition to observations by generations of hypnotists, have found that patients take in everything said around them while in the anesthetic state. Exact details and words can be recalled accurately in hypnosis. Whatever is said gets registered as a hypnotic suggestion. Sometimes careless words can be interpreted as negative suggestions. When the authority figures in surgery speak, it sets the tone for the patient's healing. Ask your doctors about what might be said. Tell them you would like to be respected as if you were hearing everything said. While you are having that conversation, be sure to ask that you *not* hear any bad news until you are fully alert. That's another good reason to be listening to music on your headphones.

The best reason to use these Healing Statements is that they make a big difference in your recovery. The evidence is very strong that patients need less pain medication, have fewer complications, and leave the hospital sooner. The statements should become standard practice in every hospital.

The second best reason to give doctors something positive to say is that it keeps their minds somewhat more concentrated on the healing aspect of the work. Operating rooms vary. In some, there's a conversational atmosphere complete with animated discussions of sports events, television shows and other chatter. In such an environment, a doctor might be having a conversation about sports and suddenly declare about an athlete past his prime: "That guy is all done. He might as well hang it up." If you're the subconscious mind of the man on the table, you might well start planning to obey the suggestion and get sicker than ever. Peggy Huddleston tells the story of a woman whose recovery wasn't going at all well, until she accessed a state in which she remembered that her surgeon had called her "a beached whale". An operating room nurse confirmed the statement.4 Some doctors remain unaware of the powerful effect of their words, which is why it's up to you and me to get them to do what we know is right. Other surgeons prefer to focus in silence. Since the words around you are so important, it's worth asking about.

Getting A Doctor to Read Them to You

It's amazingly easy to get doctors to agree. Many are immediately receptive. When a friend was in surgery for a badly broken ankle, both surgeon and anesthesiologist said yes. Then one of the nurses knew about healing statements and asked if she could read them, too. When I had eye surgery recently, the anesthesiologist was happy to read them to me. Doctors and nurses are starting to be familiar with these, but many still don't know the reasoning or research. Tell your doctor that you have read about Healing Statements spoken during surgery and you believe in the benefits. Here's all you need say:

"Doctor, there are four Healing Statements I'd like you, or Dr. _____ (the anesthesiologist), to say to me during the operation." Give your doctor a page with the statements, blanks filled in (you'll see in a moment). Then ask: "Would you say them yourself?"

It depends on the personalities involved. My observation is that the anesthesiologist says them most of the time. The anesthesiologist's position (often near your head) makes it easy to talk to you, and he or she stays tuned into your consciousness. The ideal is to have everyone on the surgical team in support. Huddleston suggests that you tape a copy to your gown (no pins, please), and that you color it brightly, which puts the whole team on notice that you have requested the reading, that it's not some strange trip the doctor is on. I suggest you type or write the statements yourself, just as you find them below. You'll own them more deeply. And decorate the paper yourself, too. Making it stand out increases the odds of the reading going well.

With the kind permission of Peggy Huddleston, here are her original, powerful, and well-tested Healing Statements, including the directions from a page intended to be a form given to the doctors. I'll explain about each of them in a moment,

"Healing Statements for Surgery

Patient's name _____

(Give this page to your surgeon and another to your anesthesiologist. Tape a third page to your hospital gown, so it is visible as you go into surgery.)

As I am going under the anesthesia, please say:

#1. **"Following this operation, you will feel comfortable and you will heal very well."** (Repeat 5 times)

After saying the statements, please put on my earphones and start my tape player.

Towards the end of my surgery, remove my earphones. Say:

#2 "Your operation has gone very well." (Repeat 5 times.)

#3. "Following this operation, you will be hungry for _____. You will be thirsty and you will urinate easily." (Repeat 5 times)

#4. "Following this operation

_____
_____
_____."

Fill in your surgeon's recommendations for recovery. (Repeat 5 times) "

Peggy Huddleston, Prepare for Surgery, Heal Faster: A Guide of Mind-Body Techniques (Cambridge: Angel River Press, 1996). Reprinted from page 257 with permission. The web site is www.healfaster.com

Here they are again, with a bit of commentary:
"**Following this operation, you will feel comfortable and you will heal very well.**"

The statement will go in deeper and deeper as you begin to move into the heightened suggestibility of the anesthetic state. If you will be conscious, have them read to you as the local is starting to work and you are relaxing. Sometimes I suggest substituting the word "procedure," which is less scary than "surgery" or "operation" when you're in a vulnerable state. Whatever language you are comfortable with and your reader agrees to.

Second Healing Statement:
"Your operation has gone very well. I am happy with your _____."

Fill in the part or area of to be worked on and healed. A deep place in your mind that has a great deal to do with your healing response will find these words reassuring. This statement helps the patient release stress at a deep level. There's almost always some holding going on, and even an anesthetized patient can feel relief and further relaxation.

Third Healing Statement:

"Following this operation, you will be hungry for _____. You will be thirsty and will urinate easily."

The idea here is to get your digestion and elimination working. This suggestion was studied at UC Davis Medical Center, where patients given such suggestions during surgery moved their bowels 1.6 days sooner than the control group. Bowel movement is one of the key indicators for recovery—and release from hospital. The elimination systems are usually slowed by anesthesia. Fill in the blank with a favorite food. Not too heavy, but almost anything is OK.

Fourth Healing Statement:

"Following this operation, _____."

For this one, you and your surgeon can come up with language that describes how recovering can and will feel for you. You're looking for clear suggestions as to how your body can feel after this specific surgery. Huddleston cites a study of patients having back surgery. The surgeon said these words during surgery:

"You will be flat on your back for the next couple of days. While you are waiting, it would be a good idea if you relax the muscles in the pelvic area, as this will enable you to urinate and it will not be necessary to use a catheter".

None of the 12 patients who heard these words needed a catheter. Five of 12 in the control group did.[5] There's a three in 1000 chance of that happening. Specific suggestions do seem to make a difference. That's why it's well worth getting the surgeon to describe the best and most comfortable recovery possible.

CHAPTER 7
Imagery, Imagination, and Hypnosis

"Man has a visible and an invisible workshop. The visible one is his body, the invisible one is imagination...The imagination is sun in the soul of man...The spirit is the master, imagination the tool, and the body the plastic material...The power of the imagination is a great factor in medicine. It may produce diseases, and it may cure them...Ills of the body may be cured by physical remedies or by the power of the spirit acting through the soul."
Paracelsus, c 1550 AD

"When every physical and mental resource is focused, one's power to solve a problem multiplies tremendously."
Norman Vincent Peale

Using Imagination for Self-Healing
The practices of Guided Imagery and Hypnotherapy have in common the intentional and conscious use of the imagination to change mental, emotional, and physical states. Images or sense impressions, pleasant or unpleasant, positive or negative, no matter what, all make something happen in body and mind. Images or suggestions speak directly to a receptive part of the mind where your creative powers reside, often called the subconscious. This activity is an ancient and normal human brain function. Everyone does it. You may recall, from a study cited earlier, that the most important factor in whether patients recovered from illness was the imagery.

Pause for a moment and think about someone you love. Did you flash on an image, an impression, or a voice, even for a split-second? Did you tune into a sound, feeling, smell, or physical sensation? A combination of sense impressions? The great benefit of imagination is that the critical factor of the mind, the part that only lets in what it already believes, is encouraged to take a rest while you allow new thoughts to reach your subconscious without being halted and searched at the border.

There are lots of people who say they can't see anything during a "visualization" or "imagery" practice. One possible reason is that most people haven't worked on this natural ability. It's like saying you can't drive a car, but you never actually learned how. It is also true that almost half the world is more tuned into touch, smell, or hearing. For them, vision isn't the top sense. That's OK, because what is often called "imagery" or "visualization" isn't so much about seeing pictures in your head as it is an exercise of the whole imagination. It doesn't matter what you call it.

Most important, it doesn't have to be complicated to be helpful. You don't have to see pictures in your head for it to work, although you probably will after a while. Staying relaxed, without trying too hard, will soon show you what you prefer, and always brings more skill and comfort. If you succeed in just going through the motions, without worrying about doing it right (there isn't any right or wrong way), you'll get the benefit, whether you notice it happening or not. And, with practice, you can hardly help getting more into it. Have faith that relaxing, imagining, and going inside yourself are skills that you will easily learn with repetition.

I'd like to invite you, just for now, to become innocent as a child and be, once again, willing to pretend. Pretend you are seeing, that you are feeling, hearing, smelling. Pretend that you are playing along in good humor. Pretending is a great thing to be comfortable about. It allows you to see new possibilities with fresh perspective. It is also one of the most wonderful and powerful of human abilities, both liberating and fun. Allow yourself to get into this scene as you read:

Pretend you are in a peaceful park, sitting, standing, or strolling comfortably, feeling safe and relaxed. Imagine the comforting sunlight filtering down through the trees, warming you comfortably. Feel it touch your skin. Look at the sky. Feel the surface under your feet, the sidewalk, grass, or dirt. Feel a gentle breeze. Hear it rustle the leaves. Imagine what smells are in the air.

See, hear, or feel anything? If you did, that's wonderful. For a lot of us, it takes a few tries. As you are reading this, bring to mind a time in the past when you felt really good: a pleasurable experience from any time in your life. Are you outside or inside? Is it day or night? Are you with someone, or alone? Bring in a few details: sounds, smells, tastes, and sensations. Notice sensations that come to you most easily. Let yourself feel really good about this moment and allow the feeling to stay with you.

While you're at it, pretend that mental imaginings really do have an effect. I don't think I can prove this to you, but I can tell you this: for thousands of years, healers, wizards, shamans, priests and priestesses in healing temples, and other wise folk in every part of the world, have believed in the power of the imagination. Almost every world-class athlete, in every sport, engages in this practice. Imagining sports performance has become a necessity. Athletes feel they cannot compete without it. Business people in corporate seminars all over the world are learning and practicing guided imagination. Why? Because they understand it gives them a performance edge.

In the first formal teaching I received in this practice, I was asked to commit to memory the following statement: *"A clear mental image tends to materialize itself as an actual condition or event."* It doesn't mean every image you see in your mind will become real on the physical plane. But the images most held in our minds, the ones that persist, tend to become a part of our lives. It's a tendency rather than a mechanical process. Pushing Button A doesn't necessarily produce Predictable Result B. We're humans, so our mechanisms can be complicated.

Since the thoughts and images we hold are so powerful, let me remind you to take a rest from violent or scary adrenaline-producing movies, at least for now. Those images persist in our minds, too. Your body is obliged to use energy to clear the adrenaline, taking something away from your healing powers. In the time before and after surgery, you are especially vulnerable to added stress, and particularly, fear-inducing "news" stories and pictures. The blatant fear mongering on television "news" programs brings stress, which might be the whole point, if you think about it. The bottom line is that stress slows down immune function and therefore delays healing. Avoiding news broadcasts will help keep your stress level down and your healing system up. Instead, have fun with this book and where it might lead you. Once you get the idea of this, there's no end to the possibilities of what you might want to imagine.

> "When I examine myself and my methods of thought, I come to the conclusion that the gift of fantasy has meant more to me than any talent for abstract, positive thinking."
> Albert Einstein

Three Fabulous Mini-Sessions

Because I want to keep life as simple as possible for you, I'll give you only three brief imagination pieces to work with. Don't be fooled. These are powerful. They will give you comfort and strength. I recommend taping them and/or taking this book to the hospital for someone to read them aloud to you. You can work with these while waiting before your procedure, sitting in the waiting room (where it will do you more good than reading magazines or taking in the tension of others), or in your room when you just want to be still.

Imagining Sunshine

The first one is a relaxed, effective and useful segment. It will take about two minutes. Just read along, eyes open, and notice what happens inside.

Right where you are sitting now, take three deep relaxing breaths. Think about being in a safe, pleasant place, maybe a nice park, a beach, or your back yard. Choose one. Without closing your eyes, just while reading this paragraph, imagine the sun warming you comfortably. Imagine yourself there. Be aware of the temperature, what kind of day it is, the time of day. Take in the physical scene, whatever is there. Look for details. Feel if there's a gentle breeze, or not. Now imagine the sun penetrating your body a little deeper, comfortably deeper, filling your whole body with its radiant light and friendly warmth. Sense the light going everywhere in your body, head to toe, arms, fingers and all. See yourself as glowing all over, perhaps more one place than others. Now imagine, see, feel the glow radiating comfortably out from your body. Imagine it moving gently with your breath. Now close your eyes and relax. See and feel yourself glowing peacefully.

It doesn't matter whether you actually "see" images clearly or "feel" the breeze. Hardly anybody does at first. The more you do it, the easier it becomes, as the pathways in your brain get familiar with this activity. It's just like learning how to ride a bicycle. Imagining light can be helpful in a dark moment. Use it whenever you like. Use it in the hospital. Use it before surgery when you have a couple of minutes to yourself. Use it while you are lying in bed. You will lower your heart rate, ease your anxiety and relax tense muscles. You can keep it simple—or you can add more relaxing breaths or your healing statements, if you like. Have fun with it. After a few times, you'll be able to do it with your eyes closed. You will almost certainly, if you practice, feel stronger and better.

The Cocoon of Light

This practice involves, as you might guess, imagining yourself in the center of a protective cocoon of light. A hospital is the right place to use it, since it brings a sense of invulnerability to influences coming at you from outside yourself. There is no shortage of germs, noises, smells, fear vibrations of others, and so on in a hospital. It's not a bad idea to have the ability to make yourself a cocoon of your own energy. There's a little more material than the others, so you may want to tape it and/or practice until you can summon it easily. Pause at each set of dots to give yourself time to allow each part to come into focus.

Begin simple diaphragm breathing until you feel yourself getting more relaxed and focused inside...Now breathe in nice and easy. Exhale. Relax now...Breathe in, Exhale. Relax now...Breathe in, Exhale. Relax now. Letting go all outer concerns for now...

Now imagine, in front of you and above your head, a bright, large sphere of light, choose any color you like. Imagine it pulsing slightly, each outward pulse sending out a wave of warm and pleasant vibrations...Notice the light beginning to spill over, flowing down over your head...your shoulders...torso...legs...your feet...

Imagine the light flowing down, now, into your head and body, flowing everywhere in you, into and between every cell, down through your feet and into the earth...Pretend that the light is illuminating darkness in your head, your heart, everywhere, and that it neutralizes tiredness and fear...Imagine that the light radiates out from you about three feet in all directions, a big glowing, softly pulsing body of light...

Entertain the possibility that love and encouragement may enter and reach your heart, while negative or discouraging thoughts bounce off your protection and return to the sender transformed into blessings...Germs and smells and unwanted sounds bounce away.

Loving and healing thoughts go in and out freely. Your loving thoughts go out and return to you after touching people you love. Now imagine thoughts of love going out to someone you care for, and returning to you. Now to someone else…and returning. Keep sending and receiving until you feel done. Now imagine others sending love and healing to you. Allow yourself to receive them. Continue breathing calmly. Take as much time as you like to open your eyes.

Imagining Excellent Recovery

This exercise first asks you to hold an image of the part of your body you wish to heal. You can look at a detailed picture or you can have the doctor draw you a sketch, or you can make up a vague representation. They are all fine. You might also want to ask your doc for a good healing image of your body. What does it look like inside when it's healing well? What does it feel like from the inside when it's going well? Write down the answers. If you don't like a suggestion, ask for another. It also works when you just make up a completely imaginary inner body landscape and imagine it being well. Your subconscious doesn't seem to be all that concerned about biological accuracy. Intention counts higher.

The second part invites you to imagine doing an activity you love. Any time you begin to worry or start to think ahead with concern, use this to focus back on the outcome you are building in your mind. Practice as many days as you can, a few minutes at a time, before your operation and for 3-6 weeks after. I encourage you to have a friend with a good voice read it to you and/or make a tape yourself. I suggest you bring it to the hospital for use as needed. Imagine it happening as a present time reality.

Begin simple diaphragm breathing until you feel yourself getting more relaxed and focused inside…Now breathe in nice and easy and deep. Exhale. Relax now…Breathe in, Exhale. Relax now…Breathe in, Exhale. Relax now. Feel the weight of your body sinking a bit into the chair, or the couch…Now conjure up an image of the part of your body you wish to see healed in the best way you can imagine. See it as knitting perfectly. Imagine it looking like what your doctor described. Imagine it feeling like it's healing well. If you see it in your mind, light up the place on your body. Let the light move around, touching each side or part of your area of surgery. See your incision looking good. Picture it fading away into healthy skin. Feel the pleasant and comforting sensations of healing. Hear your doctor's voice saying to you that your recovery is better and faster than usual, and when you hear that, you'll know it's true, because you are now tuned into your Inner Healer.

Now imagine yourself completely recovered. See yourself engaged in an activity that shows you moving really well, with ease and comfort. Walking, running, wheeling, anything you can imagine for yourself...Feel how your body feels, now that you have recovered...See how good your body looks now. How do you feel now that this episode is over? Hear your doctor's voice, now, telling you how pleased he or she is with your recovery, how wonderful and surprising that you have recovered so fast and so well...

Allow yourself to rejoice that your mind has speeded up your healing process. Imagine the joy of people who care about you that you are well now...Think of a physical activity you like a lot, and imagine yourself doing it happily...See yourself eating well, just the right things...And when you open your eyes, you feel very good.

In the days before you go to the hospital, use every opportunity to imagine yourself doing that favorite activity, or any piece of the last exercise, maybe a short clip of yourself being well in the near future. Try it in 10-15 second bursts: on waking, going to sleep, just before you leave the house, brushing your teeth, before eating, any time you are waiting in line, on the bus, everywhere. Any time you begin a segment of activity. Let those moments be cues to call a healing idea into awareness many times each day.

Guided Imagination and Hypnosis

One of the keys to imagination practice is that you enter into a different state of mind. It happened just now if you felt the sun or the light or the favorite activity. Because it takes a little learning and practice to develop the ability to go deeper, I've found that most people are able to get there faster with the help of a guide. That's where Guided Imagery and Hypnosis private sessions, tapes and CDs come in. There are several very good recordings of guided sessions. More about them in a minute.

The recordings help you get to a state in which mind and body connect and interact. Good things happen. All you have to do is lie back, close your eyes and listen. In this state, you relate directly to your subconscious, which receives the sense impressions that you accept and adopt and translates them for your body. As I said, the term 'Guided Imagery' really means a guided relaxation exercise that usually includes other senses as well. By the way, you need not worry about being controlled. You will automatically filter out any suggestion you don't accept.

The tapes I'll recommend are reliable in quality of content and presentation. Several have been proven effective in clinical studies. The advantage is that you can listen many times, enter a good state, but you only pay once. The ideal circumstance would be to have a live session, then listen to one or more of the recordings.

Find A Live Therapist

If you are aware of one and can manage it, find a hypnotherapist or Guided Imagery specialist to do one or two sessions with you. Any difference between the two doesn't matter for now, since either can do a world of good. You're looking for someone who understands what needs to be said. Even one session can relax you, improve your outlook, change your expectations, reduce your stress, and improve your outcome. I believe a session with a skilled and sympathetic operator is more effective than a tape, for two reasons: first, every person has individual concerns that can be addressed; second, in person, he or she can get you to a deeper and more receptive state where more can be accomplished. If you can't find someone who has studied the special needs of surgery recovery, you might be better off with a recording. At my website, there is a collection of reports of studies showing the significant results using hypnosis to prepare for surgery. I believe the evidence supports hypnosis as the most valuable single thing to do for yourself before surgery, if you could only pick one.

How Does It Work?

These practices are effective and valuable because, in terms of brain activity, picturing something or bringing to awareness a sense impression, and actually experiencing it, are deeply connected. Brain scans have verified this connection. Stimulating the brain with imagery can have a direct effect on the nervous and endocrine systems, as well as the immune system. If you picture yourself at the beach in a state of peace, your muscles will actually relax and your skin will feel the warmth of the sun's rays.

Many studies of athletes have shown that those who practice a skill, foul shots, for example, mentally seeing themselves doing the action, get physical benefit and improvement of skill almost as if they had done the actual activity. Pro golfers have adopted relaxation and mental imagery almost unanimously. In the same way, imagining yourself recovering quickly and comfortably from surgery makes you more likely to heal faster with ease and comfort. The brain's visual cortex, which processes images, has a powerful connection with the autonomic nervous system, which controls involuntary activities such as pulse, breathing, and physical responses to stress. Soothing, uplifting mental impressions can actually slow your pulse and your breathing and also lower your blood pressure, as well as help trigger the release of hormones such as endorphins, which make you feel good and nurture your body's restorative powers.

In the 1970s, Carl Simonton, M.D. and psychotherapist Stephanie Matthews-Simonton, created a program, now known as the Simonton method, which utilized guided imagery to help cancer patients. The patients pictured their white blood cells attacking their cancer cells. Simonton found that the more vivid the images his patients used (for example, ravenous sharks, immune cells, gobbling up weak little fish, the cancer cells), the better the process worked. Lots of gentler, less warlike, imagery has been found effective since then.

Guided Imagery and Hypnosis have been studied in hospital settings for over 25 years, and now more than ever as hospitals are realizing that their patients can get better faster. The cumulative research shows that recorded suggestion programs, whether imagery or hypnosis, are effective for:

—Increasing immune function.
—Increasing natural killer cell activity.
—Lowering complication rates.
—Reducing and stabilizing blood pressure.
—Lowering anxiety, promoting peace of mind and relaxation.
—Less pain, greater comfort.
—Lowering need for pain medications.
—Reducing depression, raising mood.
—Lowering cholesterol and blood glucose levels.
—Minimizing blood loss during surgery.
—Reducing effects of chemotherapy, especially nausea, depression, and fatigue.1

Other studies show that guided imagery is particularly helpful for patients preparing for and recovering from surgery. A 1996 study at the Cleveland Clinic, for example, showed that patients who used guided imagery before colorectal surgery had less anxiety before and less pain after the surgery than did the control group. The members of the guided imagery group used 37% less pain medication, regained their bowel function sooner, and were released from the hospital an average of a day and a half earlier.2

Here is a quick overview from an article in the *American Journal of Registered Nursing*, just so you'll get the flavor:

"Caring-healing therapies can include both visual and imagery processes to affect emotions and 'help to calm, soothe, relax, and enhance images of harmony and wholeness of being.' Therapeutic communication with guided imagery is a cognitive tool that acts as a mechanism for perceptional, emotional, and bodily change. Use of guided imagery has been promoted to facilitate the healing process; to control acute or chronic pain, both physical and psychological; and to decrease anxiety and fear. Patients undergoing elective colorectal surgery who listened to guided imagery tapes for three days before surgery, during induction, and for six days postoperatively experienced considerably less preoperative and postoperative anxiety and pain and required almost 50% less narcotics after surgery than patients in a control group. Listening to guided imagery audiotapes is a simple method to help patients use their imaginations to create images of temporary escape and relaxation that elicit a sense of well-being."3

Patients using the Simonton method have successfully used guided imagery as an adjunct therapy to conventional cancer treatments to mobilize their immune systems.

Other recent studies of guided imagery or hypnosis have found:

—Reduced pain following anorectal surgery, improved quality of sleep and decrease in anxiety.4

—The hypnosis group's wound healing was "significantly greater" compared to a supportive attention group and a standard care group by week seven after breast reduction surgery.5

—Shorter length of hospital stay after cardiac surgery, decrease in average direct pharmacy costs, higher patient satisfaction with the treatment.6

—Reduced post-surgery pain and distress after breast biopsy.[7]

—Less postoperative pain, patients coped better and requested less pain medication, were less distressed after abdominal surgery.[8]

—Reduced anxiety, more relaxed, used significantly less pain medication after coronary artery bypass surgery.[9]

—Bone fracture surgery patients had dramatically improved healing, better mobility, strength, and less need for analgesics.[10]

Keep in mind that the studies are almost always done under less than ideal conditions. For example, the people who make recordings seem to agree that you get the best results from listening twice a day for 15-20 days. In that time, you make the positive material a part of you. If you have 3 weeks, start as soon as you can and you'll do better than if you hurriedly give a quick listen the night before surgery, although even that will do you lots more good than not listening at all. Keep in mind that the studies only involve one isolated practice at a time. Think how much better off you are if you use two or three, or more, of the strategies recommended in this book.

Belleruth Naparstek has an archive at her awesome site (*Resources*) with many summaries of studies supporting the value of hypnosis and guided imagery. I recommend her tapes and CDs and especially the site itself. She has thoughtful guided material for specific illnesses and circumstances, many of which have been clinically tested. A recent study of her *Successful Surgery* set produced striking results. Here are excerpts from Blue Shield's news release:

> "SAN FRANCISCO, Jun 18, 2002—Citing strong evidence of the therapeutic and economic value of its new Guided Imagery Program for pre-surgical patients, Blue Shield of California announced the findings of a comprehensive year-long study at the recent National Managed Care Congress. The study shows that guided imagery, a simple, but powerful, mind-body technique that features the use of relaxation tapes and other imagery exercises, provides documented benefits to patients preparing for surgery, while decreasing hospital charges.
>
> According to the study, which ran from June 2000 to 2001, 57 percent of patients who listened to the audio-

recordings said they experienced less pain than expected from their surgery. Members also reported a significant reduction in anxiety after listening to the tapes prior to surgery. Forty-five percent of patients experienced high anxiety before listening to the tapes, but less than 5 percent experienced similar anxiety from listening to tapes before surgery...

Acceptance and usage of the program was high, with 85 percent of patients who used it would recommend it to a friend, and 84 percent would use it again when having surgery...Guided imagery practice sessions are short, simple to use and do not require special knowledge or equipment, enabling members to achieve meaningful results in a short period of time...75 percent of members invited to participate in the program decided to use the materials.

From the health plan's perspective, the program has proved to be extraordinarily cost-effective. The retail cost of $18 per recording nets an average hospital claim savings for billed charges of $654 per participating member."

The National Institutes of Health (NIH) has formally acknowledged and endorsed the value of relaxation and hypnosis in these words:

Relaxation: The evidence is strong for the effectiveness of this class of techniques in reducing chronic pain in a variety of medical conditions.

Hypnosis: The evidence supporting the effectiveness of hypnosis in alleviating chronic pain associated with cancer seems strong. In addition, the panel was presented with other data suggesting the effectiveness of hypnosis in other chronic pain conditions.

Conclusions. A number of well-defined behavioral and relaxation interventions now exist and are effective in the treatment of chronic pain and insomnia. The panel found strong evidence for the use of relaxation techniques in reducing chronic pain in a variety of medical conditions as well as strong evidence for the use of hypnosis in alleviating pain associated with cancer."[11]

The research shows that patients using positive visualization and relaxation techniques tend to have more positive post-surgical outcomes. Even tapes of verbal suggestions only, without imagery, played to patients while in surgery proved beneficial: *The Lancet*, a major British medical journal, reported that surgical patients who listened to audio suggestions via headphones while under anesthesia in the operating room recovered from their surgery faster than those who did not. Patients in the study underwent hysterectomies. During the procedure, they heard cassette recordings of suggestions such as, "How fast you recover is up to you—the more you relax, the more comfortable you will be," and: "The patient is fine; the operation is going well." One-half of the patients studied were released from the hospital just one day after the removal of their stitches. Only ten percent of the patients who weren't exposed to the recordings were released in that time. Patients who heard the tape left the hospital 1.3 days sooner than the other group.12

Inappropriate or misinterpreted remarks, made by doctors and staff while a patient is in the anesthetic state, and supposedly can't hear them, can have a harmful effect on recovery. It turns out that under hypnosis, patients can recall what was said while they were "out." Ask your surgeon and your anesthesiologist to avoid casual speech that your subconscious mind could interpret to your disadvantage, and ask them to use the Healing Statements from Chapter 6.

Recordings to Own

I recommend strongly that you buy one or more tapes or CDs. The best in the class known as Guided Imagery come from Belleruth Naparstek, whose tapes Blue Shield used in the above study. Belleruth's is a two-tape set with the title *Successful Surgery*. One side of Tape 1 is Guided Imagery. The other side has affirmations. Tape 2 has only relaxation music, intended for play any time, including during the operation. This set has been in many studies and the positive results are well documented.

Neil Neimark, MD has made an excellent tape that is based on the latest research. He provides a pre-surgery session that instructs your body how to act during and after surgery. It's not a fancy recording, but it is scientifically right on. Dr. Neimark cites research that shows major improvement in results when the patient has received specific instructions, as compared to simple relaxation. He maintains that simply relaxing before surgery is somewhat like an athlete relaxing for the whole time before a marathon. Surgery requires mental and physical preparation of the kind he offers on his tape. I think he's right, so I recommend you have his tape. It does marvelous things like suggest that your blood flow away from the surgical site while the surgery is going on, then return, filled with nutrients, as soon as the site is closed. Here's Dr. Neimark's quick summary of why to listen to these recordings

"Recent studies verify that listening to a properly prepared guided imagery cassette tape prior to surgery can bring about positive post-surgical outcomes in patients, including:

Decreased blood loss during surgery,

Decreased length of stay in the hospital and

Decreased need for post-operative pain medication.

Additional benefits for many patients include improved wound healing and decreased anxiety."[13]

One other very good recording I know of is titled *Healing for Surgery,* by a gifted hypnotist, Wendi Friesen. It is one tape only. The first side is 'Preparation for Surgery.' The second is 'Rapid Healing after Surgery.' I recommend listening to both sides before your procedure. Hearing the second side prepares your mind for successful recovery right from the start. I used this tape both before and after my eye operation, alternating with the others. I love the comfort and reassurance of the post-surgery sessions. There is no separate music track, but you can use any of the healing music recordings recommended in Chapter 12. Oh yes. You would expect that, having listened to all the above tapes, I would have a fast and relatively comfortable healing. I did, and yours can be too.

My recording is also good. It is available at my web site, *(Resources)*. One track is for before surgery, to prepare you mentally and emotionally, using the latest research on what works best. Track 2 is effective for after surgery to increase comfort and speed recovery.

I really hope you start listening to at least one of the recordings well before your operation. You can go to the web sites and decide for yourself. I wouldn't want to pick just one. I was lucky to have all the above when I needed them. I strongly encourage listening to a recording several times and getting comfortable with it. Then, when you are used to the style, your relaxation will probably whoosh over you as soon as you hear the first words. This form of relaxation is a skill you learn easily with practice. The people who make these recordings recommend listening every day for three weeks.

Relaxing and visualizing healing will continue to help you feel more comfortable for your entire recovery period, both in hospital (if you stay) and after you come home. Your healing ought to have this support even after you are moving around and feeling OK. The healing continues on many levels. True recovery continues for quite a while after you stop feeling the discomfort, so I recommend you allow yourself time to allow the process to unfold. You can always keep moving to beyond OK. With practice, you will be able to quickly evoke the healing feelings or images that the recordings have familiarized you with. You will be able to use these states to help yourself ease through stressful moments while you're recovering. You will also find these skills useful for helping with any health problem.

Practical Tips for Using Tapes or CDs During Surgery

Get your surgeon's permission in advance to have a small tape recorder or CD player with earphones with you. Without that advance approval the hospital staff that prepares you for surgery might take it away.

Decide what tracks or sides you want to hear. Ask the anesthesiologist, in advance, to start it and, if necessary, play another side or track. If you have auto-reverse and you want to hear both sides, set your player to do that. If you want anything more than a simple start of the recording, write a note and tape it to your playback unit. Bring an extra set of fresh batteries for surgery day.

Make Your Own Tape

If you are feeling creative, you could make your own tape. You can write your own guided imagery script, add your favorite healing statements, and read it all onto a tape. Use the scripts I have provided (the short exercises at the start of this chapter, or the long script in Appendix D), plus the healing statements from Chapter 6. Some people respond better to affirmations than to imagery. All in all, I recommend a live session, then using the tapes you can buy, supplementing them with your own creations. If you know you're going to be in hospital for a while, or recovering for more than a day or two, your own tapes can bring additional variety and a nice lift.

If you are feeling ambitious, I've included a sample script, as

Appendix D, that you can use to make your own tape. It has the basic elements. A personal session would be customized for your personality, concerns and situation, and would most likely be even more powerful, but this general script covers the main points. You can have a friend read it to you or you can tape it yourself. While it remains simpler and easier to buy a couple of the recordings I've recommended, some of you might want to know just a little more, or might not feel able to spend the money. The voices on the recordings are experienced, skilled at bringing you into a good state, which is hard to duplicate right off. Be of good cheer, though. Any reading of the script will be more useful to you than none at all, provided you play along with the suggestions.

CHAPTER 8
Prayer, Forgiveness, and Gratitude

"Pray for one another, so that you may be healed."
James 5:16

"The surest way to intensify an illness is to blame oneself or the Deity."
Norman Cousins

This chapter has two themes. The first is the value of others praying for you. The second is your own practice of prayer and forgiveness, whether for yourself or for others. If the word prayer doesn't sit well with you, I suggest you substitute the idea of transmitting healing intention. When I write of healing prayer, I am thinking of it as a support to the medical care you are getting, not a substitute. Even though much good comes from prayer, the research does not show a level of reliability that supports abandoning health professionals. Miracle healings and spontaneous remissions do occur, but not with a consistency or discernible pattern that doctors or patients can rely on. The weight of the prayer studies, though, leans strongly in the direction of improved outcomes. Odds are in your favor, even though there's no guarantee for an individual patient. The subject is wrapped in mystery and wonder.

Letting Yourself Be Prayed For

Prayer, or healing intention, conducted over distance (referred to as non-local prayer) has been shown to help people heal from surgery. Several recent studies indicate that when surgical patients are prayed for, from a distance, by strangers, without even knowing they are being prayed for, there seems to be a positive effect. Studies have found that groups of patients have had Improvement in decreased need for pain medication, fewer complications from surgery, speedier recovery and quicker departure from the hospital. A study at Duke Medical School showed, for example, that heart patients who received prayer had 50% fewer side effects than those patients not prayed for, even fewer in some groups.1

In some of the latest research, another team of doctors at Duke analyzed 150 heart patients undergoing various treatments, including angioplasties. They divided the patients into five groups. All of them received medical treatment, but four groups also got one of the following: touch therapy, relaxation training, lessons in using guided imagery or being prayed for without their knowledge. The results: patients who received any of the additional therapies were 25 to 30 percent less likely to develop complications from their medical treatment than those who received nothing extra. "We know from past studies that relaxation exercises, meditation and being gently touched and cared for can have profound effects on the heart. These activities reduce blood pressure, heart rates and stress hormones," says Harold G. Koenig, M.D., director of the Center for the Study of Religion, Spirituality and Health at Duke. "But in this case, the group with the lowest complication rates was the one being unknowingly prayed for. There's no scientific explanation for that."2

A study of 900 patients in a cardiac care unit at St. Luke's, in Kansas City, showed a difference between the prayed-for group and the group not prayed for. As is usual in this research, the patients were unaware of being in a study. The researchers found 11 percent fewer cardiac complications. In addition, the complications in the prayed-for group tended to be less serious than in those patients who weren't prayed for. What does this mean? "We don't know," says William S. Harris, M.D., Professor of Medicine at the University of Missouri, who headed the study. "At the moment, we've only shown that an association exists between being prayed for and having an improved outcome. How it works is way beyond anyone's understanding right now. But I think these studies show that research on nonphysical methods of healing is legitimate and can be done objectively and scientifically."3

Dr. Koenig cautioned: "People shouldn't stop taking any medication because someone is praying for them. Nor should doctors push religion on patients or pray with them without their requesting it. But if patients want to pray on their own, I think we should encourage it. It's also reassuring to know that if we're praying for someone to get well, we just may make a difference."4

One of the most fascinating recent studies found that prayer dramatically affects the success rate of *in vitro* pregnancies. In a study, done through Columbia University Medical School, 200 women undergoing *in vitro* fertilization in South Korea were separated into two groups: one group was prayed for by American, Canadian, and Australian Christians from several denominations, all at their own homes. The other group was not prayed for (as far as we know). No subject knew she was being prayed for. The prayed-for group had a 50 percent pregnancy rate; the group not prayed for had only a 26 percent success rate.5

The results are, as I said, for groups. When the group does better, you know that some of the people did better. But this is not an exact science. The researchers don't know how many people in the no-prayer groups had friends and relatives pulling for them. It could be that prayer is even more effective than the studies show. A good perspective on this is to realize that asking friends to pray for you, or think of you, at a certain time, may or may not "produce a result" that anyone can measure. But just think of events you've witnessed when a tiny incremental shift made a difference. Sometimes a little can change a lot.

Here's a good reason why organizing people to focus on you is a great thing: there's no risk of harm and a good chance of helping. You've got to like the odds. If you entertain the possibility that words and thoughts have real effects on visible and invisible levels, then you can easily imagine that those healing thoughts are doing some good somewhere. I like to think of it as a tonic for the spiritual atmosphere around us. When people are thinking of you, praying for you, loving you, you can be sure something is happening on the subtle planes.

Being religious is not a requirement. You don't have to be religious to give or receive prayer. You don't even have to come to grips with the world of spiritual energies. If you believe in electricity or television (once thought of as strange invisible forces), you can imagine how the power of consciously directed thought can influence external reality. It doesn't seem to matter what you believe in. The patients in the studies who receive the prayer never know they are being prayed for, so their beliefs are not examined. Albert Einstein, one of the most brilliant minds of the 20th century, is the subject of a perhaps-true tale:

—"A reporter came to visit Albert Einstein. When she arrived at his laboratory at Princeton, she was surprised to notice a horseshoe hanging above the door.

"Professor Einstein," she said, "surely a great scientist like you doesn't believe a horseshoe will bring good luck."

"Of course not," he replied. "I think that notion is utter nonsense."

"Then why is that horseshoe up there?" she asked.

"Because it works whether you believe it or not," Einstein replied."6

All sorts of prayers from many faiths seem to work, but it is a delicate subject, so researchers rarely ask about the content of the prayers. The best information is that it makes no difference what faith or religion is followed, or even that there is a formal one. No one has a monopoly on effective prayer. Ask your Support Team members to do what feels right to them. If they are accustomed to prayer, they know what to do. If not, they can perhaps find a clue or two in the rest of the chapter.

> "The imagination of man can act not only on his own body but even other and very distant bodies. It can fascinate and modify them; make them ill, or restore them to health."
> Avicenna (The foremost physician of his time, 980-1037).

Larry Dossey, MD has written several good books on the healing power of prayer, including *Healing Words: The Power of Prayer and the Practice of Medicine* and *Prayer Is Good Medicine*. Dossey makes a strong case for the effectiveness of non-local prayer. He points out that no scientist involved in prayer studies thinks that the distance between the person praying and the one being prayed for diminishes the effect in any way.

Non-local prayer seems to work even under the ridiculously unfavorable conditions of the studies (strangers praying for patients who had no idea they were being prayed for). I think it is fair to imagine that it works even better when people who love you are praying for you and you know they are. The awareness of being prayed for can hold you in a nice cocoon of safety. Carole Grant, of New York, had two groups praying on the West Coast around the time of her surgery. Her cousin, my friend Dr. Stephen Holtzman, and her daughter put them together independently.

How do you get this to happen? You ask. Who do you ask? Start with friends. Ask a close friend if he or she will help call people and set up a phone tree to remind everyone on the day of your surgery. That should be enough, but you can always add church groups as a likely source of support. Even if you aren't in a church, you know people who are—and who would be happy to ask a few others to pray for you. When a group manages to get together in one room, it seems to amplify the signal a bit, but it's not a necessary element. Being connected by phone can help unify the group, too. Look for ways to give people a sense of team effort.

Ask them simply to pray for you, or think of you with love, in their own ways. They can be anywhere in the world. Even time appears to be highly flexible. Your team can miss the time by hours and it will probably not matter. Such is the strength of energized thought through time and space. All you need to ask is that they simply hold the thought of you, perhaps even looking at your picture, with love and good wishes. They can choose any form they are happy with and direct it to you before, during, or after the scheduled time of your operation. It's hard to tell people exactly what time, as hospital timing can change, so just give your friends the scheduled time and ask them to hold you in mind and heart. Exact timing, according to Dr. Dossey, is less important than we might think. Most important, you don't have to believe anything to entertain possibilities.

Directed healing intention, or prayer, and healing circles are the most important functions of your Support Team.

Praying for Yourself: A Slightly Unusual Perspective

Most of us in Western culture have been trained to think of prayer as asking for something we do not now have from a higher power, or God, who, we are taught, often doesn't respond. Explanations often revolve around divine wrath, human unworthiness, or both. We ask for all manner of items: peace, love, money, a change of circumstance, a new house, a Mercedes-Benz. Seldom do we ask consistently, so we can't tell for sure if our prayer would have worked if we had kept at it. But many dedicated and consistent efforts at directed prayer don't seem to produce the desired result, either. Why not? What might be better, or more in tune with Divine Will, or Universal Energy, or whatever power you credit?

For example, if I were to pray, "Lord, let there be peace in the world," I am, without meaning to, most likely affirming that peace does *not* now exist. How can that be? Because the background assumption of the prayer, the dominant thought, is of the absence of peace, or more directly, the present existence of conflict. It is, in truth, the conflict that is usually most present in our minds and most intensely affirmed. A bumper sticker that proclaims "No war" is actually forcing us to imagine war, then attempt to negate it. That's how the mind works. Subconsciousness does not recognize the "no."[7]

People pray all the time for better health, while the dominant thought is actually lack of health, the mind focused on the illness ("Oh, my aching kundabuffer."). Since energy seems to follow thought and we tend to get more of what we think about, the likely result of obsessing about lack of health is more lack of health. Suppose when your focus is on the absence of something, you tend to increase the absence of that same something?

How then do we overcome this all-too-human foible? How do we pray for healing without strengthening the opposite of what we want? This applies equally to praying for our own healing or for someone else's. How about treating prayer as more a state of consciousness than a formula of words and beseechings?

Imagine entering into a state that is relaxed and focused, then concentrating on the situation or circumstances you truly want. Imagine seeing your healthy self, active and happy. Imagine it as real as you can, with sounds, sensations and feelings. Imagine that with every thought, word, emotion and sensation, you are inviting yourself to be full of the feeling of being whole and well. When such vivid imagining occupies center stage, thoughts and images of lack of wellness don't have as much room to arise. On the mental, spiritual and emotional planes, the invisible mechanism of manifestation begins to work as you ask.

Some very familiar prayer methods don't fit the model I advocate. Many "traditional" methods of prayer seem to come out of a profound sense of separateness from God, or whomever or whatever we are praying to, separateness from creation, separateness from the very condition or thing that is wanted.

I call what I'm inviting you to consider "connected prayer." In this mode, we acknowledge our unity with all creation and with divine source.

We acknowledge our connectedness to all sentient beings. We carry on with life, holding the thought that our prayer has already been answered. Allow me to suggest that you suspend your disbelief just enough to pretend it works like that. Why not become like a child, as the scripture instructs us, filled with the feeling that the desired outcome is at hand?

In this state, you're not asking a higher power to provide you with a particular result, but rather entering into a state from which the best possible results will flow, in which your body's natural healing ability will do its best. You do not need to request that a higher power remove or alleviate a particular symptom, because such a focus just brings more attention to the problem, rather than the healing. Once we ask for our aching elbows, or whatever, to be better, we are solidly focused on the hurt, not the healing. The most likely physical-world outcome would be for the hurt to persist. A short piece of dialogue from the Order Desk of the Cosmic Pain and Pleasure Center: "Hey, this customer keeps talking about aching elbows, over and over and over, let's send him a truckload this time and maybe he'll be satisfied."

Whatever you do, let me remind you to avoid using the possessive pronoun "my" in connection with anything you don't want. Use of the possessive just magnifies its attachment to you. Do, however, ask for the highest good for your whole being. Pretend that goodness and mercy follow you all the days of your life. Pretending is powerful.

The Old Stuff
Here's how most of us have been taught to pray for health:

—Focus upon the present grim reality, actually believing that health is not present for you or a part of you.

—Feel helpless, powerless or angry at events and conditions you are living with.

—Ask for intervention from a divine higher power outside yourself to bring health, still believing deep inside yourself that health is absent.

—Pray automatically or unconsciously. Unknowingly affirm the conditions that you don't want. When we say "Please let there be health for me," or for health for another, we are often declaring that health is not present in a particular situation. By concentrating on the deficit, we are increasing it. What we focus on tends to increase, even our deficits.

—Keep asking for divine intervention until you see the change occur in physical reality, thus sending an implied message of lack of faith, of mistrust in the power of effective prayer and/or the divine. It is a form of materialism, as it denies the existence of action that is not perceived by the five senses. Such a view denies the power of spiritual activity.

You Are Invited to Consider Another Possibility

Connected prayer works kind of like this. Start by using breath and relaxation to get into a good state.

—Affirm that your words and thoughts are real and powerful here now.

—Acknowledge that health is already present in your being and allow it to be there without resistance. Even if you are ill, there is some health in you, as long as you live. Give it recognition.

—Notice judgments you have on the situation or on others, releasing them by blessing the conditions that have brought pain. Blessing them does not mean agreeing or consenting to the conditions. It is acknowledging that conditions or events are part of the unity of all life.

—Cultivate the realization that a measure of change has already happened, is still happening, and will keep on happening on planes of your existence you don't see. Keep faith, whether you perceive the changes or not, by entertaining the possibility of invisible forces at work on your behalf.

—Ground and anchor your prayer with gratitude: for healing, for the opportunity to choose healing, for the opportunity to unify your life.

By putting together breathing, relaxing, and healing statements, you can put yourself in a state where connected prayer becomes possible. In a moment, I'll offer a sample. Feel free to use it or as a springboard to write your own. There are few things more powerful for your well-being than taking the time and space to write your own words. I do not want to dictate any form of praying. I offer this as one of many possibilities: one of many ways, certainly not the way.

Start with three medium-full diaphragm breaths to relax.

Try these words, or something like them. It's the point of view that counts. Read them, or your version, out loud, with feeling. Make a recording, if you like. Take a relaxing breath between each statement and let it go easily as you consider the thought.

—I, (your name), realize that my thoughts and words are real and powerful.

—I acknowledge that wellness exists now in my body; I allow myself to realize health and wellness in me; I am whole and I gladly release any resistance to health now.

—I forgive myself and I have let go of blaming myself or anyone else for conditions that have seemed to exist for me. I now send love, forgiveness, and blessing to myself, to my friends and allies, and to those whom I may have blamed.

—I realize that my prayer has already brought good change, that change is happening now, that healing energy is right now moving in me and my world, whether I am aware of it or not.

—I send forth my gratitude for the opportunity to choose a healing path with heart, for the chance to give and receive love, for friends, children, grandchildren, for this opening to bring wholeness to my life.

(Add or substitute what you feel the deepest gratitude for.)

Use a phrase of ending: *Amen...That's all, folks...Om Shanti... Thanks...So let it be...Glory...*

Pick your own word to end your ceremony. Repeat the word several times. Chant it. Sing it. Give yourself time to be still and notice that you are in a different state. Allow thoughts and feelings to come up. Make a few notes or draw a picture, if that seems right. Notice how your state has changed.

Expressing loving thoughts, such as those above, brings about instant changes in your cells. You can get a sense of how this might work from the Emoto photographs of water (*Resources*). Another lovely benefit of prayer is that it seems to be circular in nature. Your love, your caring and your good wishes go out to others and return to you in their own ways. The Dalai Lama tells us: "One of the basic points is kindness. With kindness, with love and compassion, with this feeling that is the essence of brotherhood, sisterhood, one will have inner peace. This compassionate feeling is the essence of inner peace."[8]

Forgiveness

"Letting go of regrets, resentment and the tendency to be critical is at the very heart of physical, emotional, and spiritual healing."
Joan Borysenko

It may at first seem off the subject, but there's a way to engage in forgiving that will help you do better in surgery and can help you have better health all around. Studies of people who have been in forgiveness workshops agree.

"A 1998 Stanford study of young adults who had felt hurt or offended showed that forgiveness could substantially reduce the anger they harbored. Anger has been associated with heart attack risk, and impairs the body's immune system. The notion that anger and an unwillingness to forgive can damage the physique as well as the psyche has gotten a boost from new research from the University of Wisconsin in Madison. Investigators there, who have not yet published their findings, have found that the less people forgave, the more diseases they had and the more medical symptoms they reported. 'We've been surprised at how strong forgiveness can be as a healing agent for people,' says Robert Enright, professor of educational psychology at the university who in 1985 created the country's first forgiveness research program. 'You can actually change a person's well-being, their emotions, by helping them to forgive.'"[9]

What is forgiveness? Try this definition: "the acknowledgement that no debt exists." That's the best I've heard, from Herbert Benson, president of Harvard's Mind-Body Institute.[10] It means releasing your personal connection to the anger and hurt. Even though a person has acted horribly to you and even genuinely appears to be in the wrong, you need not ruin your happiness, health, and life over that person by holding on to even quite justifiable anger at them. Forgiveness does not mean going back into a situation and setting yourself up for more bad stuff.

It does not mean pretending that something done against you wasn't really so bad, or that you caused it or brought it on yourself. You can forgive someone and still testify against him or her at the trial, describing what happened, but you don't need resentment, anger, or hate, to see justice done. Bitterness does no harm to your wrongdoer, much to you. "Hatred is a banquet until you recognize you are the main course," says Dr. Benson.[11]

What does forgiveness consist of? Most researchers agree that forgiveness is different from condoning, excusing, forgetting or denying an offense, and it does not always involve reconciliation. Forgiving and seeking justice are quite compatible. "If someone intentionally smashes your car, you can forgive them. But you can also seek payment of the bill for the body shop," says Enright. Forgiveness also does not mean putting yourself back in an abusive relationship.12

An especially important thing to know about the subject is this: *"Forgive us our trespasses (our debts) as we forgive those who trespass against us (our debtors)."* Reflect on the often-overlooked word: *as*, meaning "in like manner." We are forgiven *the same as* we forgive. Jesus spells it out clearly in the parable of the unmerciful servant.

Peter came to Jesus and asked, "Lord, how many times shall I forgive my brother when he sins against me? Up to seven times?"

Jesus answered, "I tell you, not seven times, but seventy-seven times. Therefore, the kingdom of heaven is like a king who wanted to settle accounts with his servants."

I encourage you to look up this story in Chapter 18 of the Book of Matthew to fill out the details of how it went for the one who had been forgiven his debt, but would not forgive another (jail and torture are mentioned). Jesus comments: "This is how my heavenly Father will treat each of you unless you forgive your brother from your heart." (Matthew 18: 21-35 NIV) No fooling about this subject.

How does one go about forgiving? If you are aware that significant old anger or resentment is still with you, I recommend working with a counselor, hypnotherapist, or spiritual advisor to let go of allowing someone else to control and ruin your life and health. Holding on to anger and resentment harms the health and the character of the holder. It does the creep who did you wrong no harm at all. Speaking to one of his forgiveness classes, Professor Fred Luskin of Stanford put it bluntly: "Why do we allow someone who's nasty to us to rent so much space in our minds?"13

It follows that successful healing after surgery is improved when we release old emotional material: anger, resentment and the like.

But consider this: trying to forgive while going over the wrongs done to you just dredges up the whole nasty business all over again. The way the mind works, you have to be thinking about what you're forgiving, and in the process you're stuck with reliving the pain. But forgiveness can't come from this place of pain. Now the question can be framed like this: how do we go about moving from a feeling of righteous anger to one that promotes our well-being without the agony? The most liberating thing to do is forget it. When you are done with the trial, the hearings, whatever outer activity is involved, release it. Let go of it to the extent that if it's a memory, it's a dim one. If there was a valuable lesson in an incident, keep the lesson and forget the circumstance. Your brain is capable of acting on your intentional message to forget.

One step is to let go of the anger and hurt. Release it. Say goodbye. Let yourself consider that no debt now exists. Even if there's money involved or some other "serious" matter for which you expect compensation, don't ruin your life. If something comes of this, wonderful. You might be surprised how often this works. Sometimes life can be simpler than you expect.

And try this: write and/or say out loud, with feeling, the following healing statements. Use one or two you like and leave the rest, or read them all to yourself out loud. Make up your own or change the wordings so you feel good about what you are telling yourself. Keep your statements in the present.

—Releasing and forgetting connects me to inner peace.
—I forgive myself for mistakes I have made that hurt me or others.
—I release my parents. They did their best.
—I release anyone who betrayed me.
—I let go of those people who have offended me.
—I let go of all unpleasant incidents that come to mind now, since they have come up for release. I have no further need to remember them.

You can allow this process to be as real and as profound as you like. I can tell you with certainty that old stuff can and does release easily and simply when we intend it deeply. Remember to listen for your inner response as you write or say each statement. Take note of what comes up for you. These statements are intended to bring feelings into your present awareness, so please give yourself the joy of going slow and allowing yourself to feel. If you like it, put them on tape, leaving pauses for reflection.

If you're feeling ambitious about this, by which I mean you'd sincerely like to be released from old pain, anger and grief that you are holding against individuals (or groups), work the following ceremony:

Go, alone if you can, to a place with moving water: a stream, river, or ocean. Take a small pail of stones if there are none there, maybe 15 or 20. Stand by the water. Take out one and pretend it carries the energies of a trespass against you. Throw it in the flowing water while saying, "I release you," or "you're *gone." Imagine the energies being carried away so they become dim and distant, eventually to fade away completely. Repeat until you can't think of anything or anyone else or you run out of stones. Breathe.*14

Expect to feel a weight lift off you. You can also do this in your imagination, but it's not usually as strong as actually throwing the stones. Losing the old resentments, as I said, helps your recovery process. Plus, it makes the rest of your life better. Successful forgetting opens the door to fresh experience.

Prayer Lists

It may do you good, and certainly no harm, to put your name on a list of people being prayed for. You can do this at your own church, if you have one, or use the general good will of many faiths and denominations. There are many people in the world with love in their hearts, willing to give to others. You may be connected to prayer circles or boards in your own church. If not, you'll find suggestions in the *Resources* section, Appendix C.

CHAPTER 9
Foods and Nutritional Supplements for Healing

"Use three Physicians—
Still-first Dr. Quiet,
Next Dr. Merryman,
And Dr. Dyet."
Regimen Sanitatis Salernitanum, Edition of 1607

"Let food be thy medicine, and let thy medicine be food."
Hippocrates

This chapter contains recommendations for:
　—What to eat in the period before surgery to allow your body to be ready.
—Supplements to make your immune system stronger before surgery.
　—What to eat after surgery in the hospital and at home for faster recovery
　—Supplements that can aid recovery.

What you take into your body for the few weeks before a surgical procedure will affect your recovery, for good or ill. Repair of your body requires a lot of energy: You can give yourself an advantage by raising your cellular nutrition a level or two. When all your body systems are nourished, your healing system works better. When your healing system works better, you will probably recover faster and be less likely to have complications or catch something in the medical facility.

This is about improving immune function by lowering stress. Stress reduces immune function. Most people think of stress as their boss yelling at them, but it's also the case that lots of things, including some foods, put stress on the system. Why force part of your healing system to work off the added stress that can come from hard-to-digest foods when it needs to focus on recovery? If you are feeling heavy from certain foods, your system is sluggish. When you feel light, you're helping yourself. It is OK to eat well and plenty, but not so much as to feel heavy. The bottom line is that certain foods and supplements will help you heal while some kinds of food would hinder your healing if you were to indulge in them.

Research shows you can speed your healing time by making a few changes. Don't worry. I'm not asking you to give up anything. Well, hardly anything. If your doctor has specific wishes, however, follow them. Here's what I do suggest: add some things to your diet that will help you have an easier time all around and lighten up on some other things that get in the way of your body's ability to heal itself. This is not a major overhaul of your habits and preferences, just a little nudge in a healing direction. I hope you do not try to make major changes, which could be stressful, at least not until you are well recovered. My purpose is to help you build up your internal strength and ease some of the stress that is always part of the medical process. I urge you to go over the following recommendations with your doctor.

I hope that, as you heal, you'll decide that you would like to be healthier for the rest of your life. Many of us could stand to eat better as part of getting healthier. If you do decide to turn this time into an opportunity to make some changes, I recommend a book as your guide: *8 Weeks to Optimum Health*, by Andrew Weil, MD, the easiest, most sensible method I know to move yourself gently along the path to more wellness. The *Resources* section has other sources of nutrition information.

Before Surgery
Foods to Have More of

Add some of these to your diet every day, whether you have 2 days or four weeks to get ready. Choose from:

Kale, Swiss chard, Spinach.
Green and Red Cabbage.
Broccoli, Cauliflower.
Red and Green Lettuce, Romaine Lettuce.
Endive, Chinese Cabbage, Bok Choy.
Edible Seaweeds.
Celery, Cucumber.

Zucchini, Brussels Sprouts, Bean Sprouts.

Sunflower Seeds.

4-5 servings daily total. The more dark green foods you eat, the better. Dark green vegetables are a great help. Some people swear by powdered dark green formulas as a good way to get what you need. I have seen some good ones, with the nutrient content of four-six servings of dark greens in a spoonful.

One of the most important aspects of surgery recovery is to get and keep your elimination system working. Having a bowel movement sooner than average after surgery is not only a sign of recovery, but you feel a lot better. You may have gotten out of the habit of eating vegetables (or never got into it), but your body loves you when you do. Greens may not be your favorite things, but you'll appreciate them when you realize that the fiber and nutrients in them help your digestion and elimination. That goes for fruit, too.

Probiotics

Any time you take antibiotics, I strongly urge you to add probiotics to your life. These are essential friendly bacteria that your body needs in your intestines. Antibiotics destroy friendly bacteria, those you need in order to digest food and otherwise function optimally, as well as the unfriendly bacteria they are meant to kill. Ask at any health food store for *Lactobacillus Acidophilus* with *Bifidobacteria* and *Lactobacillus Bulgaricum*. These three protect your intestinal tract, helping prevent bad effects of antibiotics, such as the diarrhea, bloating, indigestion and other problems that arise from not having sufficient friendly bacteria. Or you can just ask for a good probiotic. They will know what you mean. You will feel miles better by taking this simple step. Also at the natural foods store is a substance known as FOS, which stands for Fructo-oligosaccharide, which helps the healthy bacteria flourish. It is considered a prebiotic. It is a wonderful addition to the probiotics. Ask your doctor if you have questions.

Fruits to Have More of:

Grapefruit, Lemon, Apples, Berries, Cherries, and Grapes. Stewed prunes are good for helping keep things moving. You are lucky if you love them. Go very light on fruit juices and sweet fruits, as even natural sugars can slow the healing function by depressing neutrophils. Vegetable juices are better.

Three or four servings of fruits daily, fresh and in season, if possible.

Try these Legumes:
Black beans, Lentils, Peas.

Have Quality Protein:
Adequate protein intake is essential for tissue repair. A minimum of 50 grams a day and as much as 80 grams a day of protein may be necessary, depending on the surgery you will have and how big and/or active you are. According to an article in the pharmacists' journal *American Druggist*, 25% of all entering patients in US hospitals were found to be protein-deficient in a 1994 study.1 The article states: "This condition significantly lengthens the time of inflammation and impairs revascularization and remodeling during the healing process." One week of protein supplementation before surgery produced a substantial improvement in wound healing, according to a study cited in the article.2

Figure about 20-25 grams of protein for a chicken breast or 4-5 ounces of fish. You don't need tons. Moderation is fine. Because meat takes more energy to digest, it's best to have smaller amounts at one time, spread out in soups and dishes mixed with vegetables. That's what most Asian cuisines do. Protein amounts are on the labels of powders, cottage cheese, soy products, yogurt and everything else packaged. Good sources are:

—Organic eggs

—Meats: game, turkey, chicken

—Deep water fish (salmon, halibut).

—Sunflower, pumpkin, sesame seeds.

—Nuts: small amounts of raw cashews. Brazil nuts, almonds, pecans.

—Yogurt with acidophilus.

—Cottage cheese.

—Soy products. Most people do well eating soy. You probably know if you don't. Soy is a good protein source.

—Whey or soy protein powder (whichever you prefer) can make a good smoothie mixed with water and fruit slices. Pineapple is good for this, especially if you can get it fresh. Most hospitals have blenders available to patient helpers. When you discover how to make something you like, you can give yourself a helpful protein supplement and feel light. Plus, you have a way to get the protein you might need for the week before surgery.

More Liquids

—Filtered water or tested well water. A minimum of one ounce daily for every two pounds you weigh. For example, if you weigh 160, that's a minimum of 80 ounces, more in summer or if you do physical work. Not bottled, not tap, not distilled. For more water information, see Chapter 10. A well-watered body heals better.

—Juices: Lemon juice and warm water on rising; grapefruit, fresh vegetable juices (carrot and celery, carrot and spinach or kale or chard). Lucky you if you have a juicer, since the nutrients are at their peak for only a few minutes.

—Green tea is good for you in moderate quantities (2-3 cups in a day). I like Shipibo Tea, a pleasant and very healthy drink made from Amazon herbs. You can drink as much of this excellent immune-builder as you like.

Foods to Have Less of For 2-3 Weeks Before Surgery

The main thing is moving toward easing up the effort your body requires to eat heavy food or metabolize fats and high-glycemic carbohydrates. These foods, and others listed below, promote the formation of free radicals, which inhibit cellular repair. These foods make your body work harder to metabolize them, which tends to subtract from energy you need for healing. Do not try to give up anything now. Moderation is in order.

—Sugar, aspartame (Nutrasweet or Equal). Certain artificial sweeteners are seriously toxic. Do yourself a favor and eliminate them from your house and your life. If you suffer from low energy, loss of muscle control, loss of nervous system control, or general aches in muscles and joints, eliminating aspartame might make you feel better as soon as it detoxes from your body, in about 3-4 weeks. Your body will take a lot of abuse, but the effects of this junk will show sooner or later when your endocrine system has gone haywire. Aspartame makes up approximately

75% of all the complaints received by the FDA. It is suspected of being a cause of several mysterious illnesses. Try life without it and see how you feel.

—High-glycemic carbohydrates (Refined carbs, such as donuts, pastries and cookies).

—Alcohol, caffeine. Both of these dehydrate your body too much for now.

—Fried foods. They increase inflammatory response throughout the body. The sagacious and nearly immortal pitcher Satchel Paige, who played major league baseball into his sixties, used to say "Don't look back, something might be gaining on you and don't eat fried foods, they heat up the blood." That's right, according to Traditional Chinese Medicine.

—Known or suspected personal food allergies. The usual suspects are milk, wheat, and corn.

—Hydrogenated oils, margarine. These trans-fatty acids slow down your healing system.

—Artificial food additives and artificial preservatives, especially MSG. These are over-stimulating.

Vegetables To Have Less Of:
—Iceberg lettuce. Almost no nutritional value.
—Fried potatoes. Deep-fried fats increase inflammation.
—Corn. Also popcorn, chips, corn flakes. Corn is really a grain, not a vegetable and is hard to digest. Whole, unchanged kernels are frequently seen in the toilet. Corn is also one of the most common allergens.

Protein Sources to Have Less of:
—Pork. In all its forms: ham, bacon, chops, roast, chitlins, tripe. A Chinese healer told me that healers cannot work as effectively when they have eaten pork. This can apply to self-healing as well. Pretend you believe it for a couple of weeks.

—Milk. Everyone who is not Northern European loses the ability to digest milk at 2 years old. It just glugs up the system for most other folks. The milk ads are nonsense for everyone without the Northern gene variant. Skim milk is no better. Get Vitamin D from an hour a day in sunshine. The dark greens listed above are much better sources of calcium for most of the world's people.

—Shellfish: Shrimp, Crab, Lobster, Clams. Traditional Chinese healers say these make the organs and the blood excessively hot, which increases the inflammation response. More inflammation is just what you don't need now.

—Peanuts. They promote inflammation a little too much for now. Your body would prefer to have a moderate, normal healing response.

Liquids to Have Less Of:

—Tap water, unless yours is good or you can't otherwise get good water. See Chapter 10.

—Distilled water. It is lifeless and leaches minerals from your body.

—Softened Water: People who drink soft, or softened, water are more likely to have heart problems. Softened water is for washing clothes and dishes in hard water areas. Hard water, which contains Magnesium and Calcium salts, is better for your insides.

—Coffee and standard tea. These are diuretics. They take water from your body. Your body must be hydrated to heal right.

—Soft drinks, especially diet drinks. For each ounce of caffeinated soft drink (or coffee) you have, subtract that amount from the water you have taken in. For example, if you have drunk 60 ounces of water, plus one 12-ounce soft drink and one 12-ounce coffee, that makes 60 minus 24. Your effective useable water intake turns out to be 36 ounces. It is not true that soft drinks hydrate you as well as water. The studies claiming that are sponsored by the industry and are not credible..

—Store-bought fruit juices usually contain excessive fructose, which slows down your body's ability to heal.

Remember, I'm not asking you to give up anything, except maybe the artificial sweeteners. I'm not a food fanatic and I don't expect you to be. The idea is to lighten up on the heavy stuff and add fruits and vegetables. You'll feel lots better.

> "I read a book about the evils of drinking, so I gave up reading."
> Henny Youngman

Supplements to Take Before Surgery

The purpose of supplements at this point is simple: to maximize the strength of your healing system *before* an onrush of challenging events related to surgery. The germs are there, the atmosphere is intense, and surgery takes a lot out of us, even so-called "minor" surgery. The more immune strength, the better off you are: you will be more likely to have a good outcome with no complications and less likely to catch something you don't want.

I'll present you with some well-accepted strategies recommended by many doctors who seem to know the most about the subject. As with foods, you decide what feels right to you. Whatever you choose to take, start two to six weeks before surgery, depending on how much time you have, and continue for at least four weeks after. You're not healed just because you can move around. Respect the time it really takes. Being a healing hero is a booby prize. The body can suffer long-term consequences if you make it do things it's not ready to.

Vitamins

First in importance is a group of standard vitamins that our bodies require for optimal healing. There's nothing fancy or unusual about this list. These nutrients provide your body with the basics. People who follow a sound program of supplementation before and after surgery typically heal faster than normal, with less pain, less swelling, and fewer complications. With supplements and herbs, however, you need to be aware that there is no certainty you are actually getting pure products, or the amounts claimed on the label. If you know and trust a source or brand, use those. I recommend no particular brand in this book because the supplement market changes quickly. At my website, I recommend the best I can find in a changing market.

If you are now happy with what you have, stay with them and adjust the amounts so that you are getting all or most of what's listed below. The list is drawn from the advice of several Chiropractors, Naturopaths, and Medical Doctors, especially Alan Gaby MD, Robert Myers ND, Jonathan Wright MD, and Andrew Saul, PhD.3 There's wide agreement about which vitamins generally help.

Check in with your doctor, as you may have personal medical requirements. Patients taking blood-thinning medications, for example, should not have much Vitamin K, which thickens blood. Expectant mothers or people with liver issues need to be careful about Vitamin A.

A message that needs repeating: Tell your doctors, especially your anesthesiologist, every supplement and every medication you are taking. Bring them all in their original containers. You need to make sure there's no conflict with a medication. To get a confident attitude about your vitamins, be sure to read Dr. Saul's article at the end of this chapter. If your doctor asks you to stop vitamins before your operation, ask for the reason. Most vitamins will not affect your surgery, but some could and you do want to know what they are.

The following are known to be helpful both before and after surgery, unless your doctor indicates otherwise. They are best taken with food:

—**Vitamin C**, 1000 mg, 8-12 times a day or more. Several experts say that Vitamin C does more to get your body ready for surgery than any other single nutrient. Just so you'll know these amounts are reasonable, Dr. Andrew Weil, at his website (www.askdrweil.com), recommends up to 20 grams a day in preparation for surgery. To be on the safe side, work up to these amounts over several days. You can easily tell when you are going too fast with Vitamin C, as your bowels will become loose. If that happens, there's no danger. It's a signal that you have reached the right amount for you. Back off just a little. Dr. Weil recommends intravenous Vitamin C and says that every surgeon who has agreed to try it has been happy with the results.[4] Talk about this with your doctor.

—**Vitamin A**, 10,000-20,000 IU a day. Speeds up healing when you take it for seven days before surgery. It helps ease post-surgical suppression of immune function and increases the strength of the scar.[5]

—**Vitamin B Multiple Complex**, which should include, in addition to all the B vitamins, at least some of the following:

—**Vitamin K**, 20-30 mcg.

—**Folic acid**, 400-600 mcg. Folates (and Vitamin B-12) stimulate growth of DNA for formulation of new cells.

—**Copper**, 2 mg.

—**Zinc** (up to 30 mg a day), Zinc levels decline dramatically during the period around surgery, burns or injury. Zinc helps strengthen new tissue. "Zinc deficiency compromises the immune system, delays closure of wounds and ulcers, and causes newly produced collagen to have a weaker tensile strength."[6]

—**Arginine** "functions as an antioxidant to kill bacteria and increase T-cell mediated activity, which, in turn, enhances immune function. Supplementation with arginine has been shown to significantly increase the amount of collagen deposited into a wound site during the healing process."7

Get a first-rate anti-oxidant formula that has many effective ingredients such as Green Tea, Alpha-Lipoic Acid, Selenium, n-Acetyl-Cysteine, Grape Seed, and anti-oxidant vitamins (E and C) in proportion. Blueberries and cranberries are among the best natural anti-oxidants. This group of nutrients minimizes free radical damage at the injury site and improves both circulation and the strength of new tissue.

Taking complete multi and anti-oxidant formulas together provides most of the list above in the right amounts. Add a good Vitamin C from a health food store, plus the arginine and zinc, and you have a good program. This is a relatively uncomplicated way to get what you need and should make a difference for you. Do not underestimate the power of simple Vitamin C.

If you add one more thing, consider L-glutamine, which, because of its effectiveness as a nitrogen donor and as a precursor for protein and nucleotide synthesis, is important for rebuilding wounded tissues.8

Here is sensible advice from Dr. Weil on the question of what *not* to take before surgery:

"If there isn't enough time to stop taking your supplements prior to surgery, bring your products to the hospital in their original containers so the anesthesiologist can see the exact ingredients in the products you're taking…Surgeons routinely instruct patients to stop taking aspirin or any other anticoagulant prior to surgery. I think it is wise to discontinue certain supplements prior to surgery—don't take high doses of garlic, vitamin E, or ginkgo, for instance. All of these have some anticoagulant effect that could pose bleeding problems during surgery…In the meanwhile, I think a more important take-away message here concerns the doctor-patient relationship. I can't stress the importance of being able to talk to your doctor openly. If for some reason you don't feel comfortable, or if you don't share the same philosophies for managing your health, you may want to look for a new doctor."9

In-Hospital Recovery (Don't Eat Their Food)

Hospital food has been notoriously poor in living up to its ideal-world aim of supporting recovery. It's appalling that hospitals seem to have few ideas and less information about foods that heal. As you might guess, large manufacturers of processed food finance and influence the education of nutritionists, so you are more likely to see food *products* than real food. If the hospital serves you items that are on the list of "Foods to Have Less Of," their food will just be a hindrance to your healing. That's often the state of things in hospitals. It is beyond belief that heart patients often get milk and pastries and other high-fat foods. Similar atrocities are abundant, although some hospitals are finally starting to improve what they offer. You could get lucky. Check what they offer against the above lists.

Make it a task for your Support Team to find out what is served in your hospital. If the hospital food is not mostly from the list of "Foods to Have More Of," plan for your Support Team to bring what you need. By doing this, you remove the possible risk of any hospital pathogens (nasty bacteria and viruses) that might get to you through the food. A strong immune system can brush aside the sneezes of a food preparer or the germs in the air, but the same germs are a greater challenge when you are not at full strength.

If you possibly can, have your own food brought to you before you are hungry, so the hospital's offerings don't tempt you. This is one of the major tasks of your Support Team. Look again at Chapter 2 for suggestions about how to get your Support Team to do things for you.

As soon as you are allowed to take liquids, focus on items that help bring your body into balance: unsweetened lemon juice and good water, diluted grapefruit juice, diluted vegetable juice, and chicken-vegetable soup or Bieler's Soup (recipe follows), especially, which feels reassuring, exactly the right thing to have as a first food after an operation.

Foods with lots of vegetables help soften and evacuate your bowels faster and more easily than most hospital foods, which can be constipating. You need healthy fiber. And, unappealing a subject as it may be, the first bowel movement after surgery is an indicator for getting out of the hospital. You'll feel better, too.

When you are ready for solid foods, focus on the good list, especially the dark greens and fresh vegetable soup, with pieces of lean meat, if you like. Eat some raw veggies and fresh fruit. Take in more good food and you'll have less desire for the foods that take away your energy. It's OK to give yourself a treat or two or three. Comfort is good.

Soups to Have More of:

—Miso, Chicken, Barley, Vegetable, especially fresh, including leafy greens.

Chicken soup is a terrific healing food. According to Hanna Kroeger's *Ageless Remedies from Mother's Kitchen,* chicken soup is a healing food because it "has a natural ingredient which feeds, repairs and calms the mucous lining in the small intestine…heals the nerves, improves digestion, reduces allergies, relaxes and gives strength." Let your Support Team bring it to you. You can also mix it with:

—Bieler's Soup. Dr. Bieler was a well known natural medicine guru for Hollywood's stars in the 40's, 50's, and 60s and created a soup that helps neutralize the intense acidity of the residue of pharmaceuticals and helps flush the waste products from your system. Finding out about this recipe was the original inspiration for writing this book. It has been helpful over the years. It is easy to digest. Digestion takes a lot of energy you could use for healing. It is a good remover of toxins. It is wonderful and valuable, I'll give you the recipe here.

Zucchini

Green beans

Celery

Parsley

Olive oil

Clean, chemical-free water

Cut up equal amounts of zucchini, green beans, and celery (fresh, preferably). Chop the celery 1/2 inch or less to eliminate stringiness.

Steam until soft. Use clean water (carbon filtered).

Fill blender 1/2 full with the vegetables and water used for steaming. Add a small handful of chopped parsley. Blend to a consistency of pea soup.

Add a small amount of olive oil.

For variety, add garlic, onions, cayenne pepper, ginger, herbs, etc. We like an ounce or so of chopped burdock root. Season with tamari or soy sauce.

Vitamins ASAP after Surgery:

The doctors mentioned above recommend that you start taking the same vitamins as before, especially Vitamin C (since surgery depletes the body's supply) as soon as possible, with the following additions:

—Bromelain capsules: Take for 2 days before and 10 days after surgery. Bromelain lessens swelling and inflammation by digesting away tissue debris. Studies show shorter healing times. (2,000 mcu/g), 250 mg, 2-3 capsules, 3 times a day on an empty stomach).

—Gotu Kola (Centella Asiatica) shortens healing time and strengthens healing tissue.

—Vitamin E. 400-800 IU, once a day. Vitamin E, in the presence of Vitamin A, speeds up wound healing and helps reduce scar formation and adhesions. Best advice is to not take Vitamin E for at least a week before surgery, due to its blood-thinning properties, as noted in Dr. Weil's comment. Dr. Petry reminds me that Vitamin E may delay collagen healing, especially in tendons. Ask your surgeon.

—Zinc chloride ointment or spray reduces the size of the wound and shortens healing time, even in patients who are not zinc deficient.

Homeopathy

Homeopathics are harmless and do not interfere with any surgical procedures or medications. They cannot have any bad effect. Consult your doctor. The following two have been widely used:

—*Arnica montana*, 100-200c, 4-5 pellets under the tongue every 30 minutes as soon as possible after surgery for 6 hours. Then 4-6 times a day for a week. Many people I know have used this successfully to help reduce soreness, bruising, tissue damage, swelling, and bleeding during recovery from surgical procedures. *Arnica* is also good to take the night before an operation.

—*Hypericum perforatum*, 100-200c, every half hour after surgery, alternating with the Arnica, is a traditional remedy for lessening pains and speeding the healing process of cuts and puncture wounds. I just used this combination after my recent surgery,

A list of possible homeopathic remedies for many specific circumstances is at www.healthnotes.com. If you know a health practitioner with homeopathic knowledge, consult her or him for more specific remedies.

Stay on the supplement program for 4-6 weeks after surgery. It takes more time to recover fully from any surgery.

An Informative Article

I am including, as a sort of appendix to this chapter, this encouraging article with practical tips from an excellent advocate of nutritional therapy. It is so right and charmingly said that I want to include the whole thing. Visit Dr. Saul's informative web site: www.doctoryourself.com, for access to a vast amount of information on vitamins and other self-healing resources. The site has abundant evidence, especially, of the high value and healing power of Vitamin C and helpful hints about how to get what you need.

"Vitamins in Hospitals: The Final Frontier, by Andrew Saul, PhD

Some things are known to just not mix. There's oil and water, and then there's hospitals and vitamins.

A hospital, by definition, is a collection of the sick, the injured, the infirm, and the stressed. All these situations call for larger than the normal quantities of dietary vitamins. When is the last time you saw a hospital or nursing home routinely give even a daily multivitamin, let alone specific high-dose therapeutic supplements?

This can immediately change, and you can help do it. Prepare to stand firm on what is most important, and negotiate the rest.

1. If you want to take your vitamins while hospitalized, bring them with you. A written statement from your doctor that you will be doing so may save a lot of fuss. I'm not exaggerating: hospital staff often tell patients they may not take anything that the hospital didn't authorize them to take. You can hardly count on them to provide megadoses of vitamins. So it is a bit like a movie theater telling you that you can't bring in your own popcorn, but they won't sell you any, either. Vitamins are vastly more important to an enjoyable hospital stay than popcorn is to a movie.

2. If you are given a plausible medical reason why you should not take vitamins, be bold and ask for written references. Look up each surgical procedure or medicine you are offered. Is there REALLY a problem with a vitamin? Complete information on drugs is contained in the PHYSICIANS' DESK REFERENCE (PDR), found in any hospital pharmacy, library

or doctors' lounge. Your public library will probably even look it up for you if you telephone them from your room.

The PDR lists all prescription medications (and there is another book for nonprescription medicines) with all their side effects, contraindications and any nutrient-drug interactions. It is quite rare for a vitamin to interfere with a prescription drug. Any such caution is in the PDR in writing. The same information is on drug package inserts. Do not assume that you doctor or nurse has memorized the nutrient/drug connections of some 3,000 drugs in the PDR.

Surgical information may be obtained from sources other than your surgeon. Try the public or hospital library for the non-technical *Good Operations, Bad Operations* by Charles Inlander (Penguin, 1993)...By the way, any doctor or nurse who makes fun of you for being thorough probably should be more thorough themselves. Don't stand for harassment, especially when you are in the right. Tell a supervisor.

Unacceptable Reasons for Stopping Vitamins:

a. "Vitamins will interfere with your tests." Just have the words "takes vitamins" added onto any paperwork. Interpretation can readily be made. If there is a specific and essential test or procedure that clearly requires suspension of vitamin supplements, you can stop the day before and resume when your doctor says OK. This way you only lose a day or two.

b. "Vitamins will be dangerous after surgery." Since all nutrition textbooks indicate a substantially increased need for vitamins during wound healing, this is illogical. Some patients have been told that their blood-thinning medications (like Coumadin brand warfarin) are incompatible with vitamins, especially K, C and E.

Vitamin C may lessen clotting time, and vitamin E may increase it. Taking both allows the body to achieve a natural balance. If you are given Coumadin, your prothrombin time should be monitored. Since they are constantly taking blood for some reason or other anyway, your "pro-time" can be checked often. Instead of reducing your vitamins, doctors can simply adjust the amount of their drug.

c. "Vitamins are unnecessary if you eat right." I say, long hospital stays are unnecessary if they FED you right. Since they don't, supplements are the simple answer. If you find a hospital that feeds you a vegetarian, three-quarters raw food diet (blended or juiced for some patients, as needed) then I will lighten up. Until then, "hospital food" will continue to deserve its almost pathogenic reputation, and supplements are completely justified.

It may be their building, but it is your body. Hospitals provide essential services and save lives. They will save even more when they fully utilize megavitamin therapy."

(Reprinted with permission from the DOCTOR YOURSELF NEWSLETTER and the http://www.doctoryourself.com website. Copyright 2003, 1999 and previous years Andrew W. Saul, 8 Van Buren Street, Holley, New York 14470. All rights reserved. Email: d rsaul@doctoryourself.com. Andrew Saul, PhD, is Contributing Editor for the Journal of Orthomolecular Medicine. *He is the author of* "DOCTOR YOURSELF: Natural Healing that Works.*)*

CHAPTER 10
The Value of Water

"Water is the only drink for a wise man."
Henry David Thoreau

"When drinking water, think of its source."
Chinese Proverb

Why You Need Water to Recover

Your body needs to be watered to heal well from surgery. Inadequate hydration stresses all the muscles and tissues. When your procedure is complete, you need a healthy supply of blood to return to the area of your surgery. The flow of blood carries oxygen and the nutrients your body needs in order to do the repair work efficiently. Blood is about 80% water. Water is a solvent for the products of digestion, helps them pass through the absorbing walls of the intestinal tract into the blood stream and ultimately to the tissues. Metabolic waste products are diluted, also, and carried into the pathways of elimination. When you are properly hydrated, efficient detoxification of the body occurs naturally.

Water is also essential as a body lubricant for various organs. Mucus, which lubricates the digestive tract and the respiratory tract, and saliva, which makes it possible for us to swallow food, require plain water to do their jobs. I realize mucus and saliva are not exactly the most delightful subjects, but it helps to be conscious of these vital body functions. By drinking adequate water, you flush out toxins and body waste products. Plus, you flush out bladder, kidney, and other urinary tract infections. A thorough article from *The American Druggist* offers well-documented support:

"People who suffer from wounds can actually help speed their own recovery without exerting much effort. As adequate hydration is crucial in wound healing, people should be encouraged to drink two to three quarts of quality water daily during the healing process. Nutrient delivery, tissue repair, detoxification and pain are all directly influenced by hydration, and injury and wound healing greatly increase the body's need for water. Factors that maximize circulation will also enhance nutrient delivery and waste removal during a time of healing."[1]

To emphasize the point again: you must be well hydrated before and after any and all surgical procedures in order to heal well. Please do this as far in advance as possible, not the day before the operation. You can make a huge contribution to your health by staying hydrated forever.

Water makes up about two-thirds of your solid body tissue (muscles) and 75 percent of your brain. It helps regulate body temperature. It carries nutrients and oxygen to cells, removes waste, cushions joints and protects organs and tissues. Your bones are one-quarter water. If you dehydrate a muscle by only 3%, you cause an approximate 10% loss of contractile strength, and 8% loss of speed. Even mild dehydration slows down the metabolism by as much as 3%; and a 2% drop in body water triggers fuzzy short-term memory, trouble with basic math and difficulty focusing on the computer screen or the printed page.

The most elaborate dietary regimes and costly nutritional supplementation can only work if a person is well watered, just as in the garden. Water is not exactly a radical idea. To show you the direction of mainstream thinking, here are recent guidelines from a well-known medical center:

> **"Your Need For Water**
> By Barbara Levine, RD., PhD., Director of the Nutrition Information Center at the New York Hospital-Weill Medical College of Cornell University.[2]
>
> Next to oxygen, water is the human body's most important nutrient. Yet 75 percent of Americans are chronically dehydrated and fail to drink the eight, 8-ounce servings of water per day recommended by health and nutrition experts.
>
> **Here are the facts on why it's important to ensure you're properly hydrated.**
> —Water plays a vital role in regulating body temperature, transporting nutrients and oxygen to cells, removing waste, cushioning joints and protecting organs and tissues.

—Water's ability to dissolve a multitude of substances allows our cells to utilize valuable nutrients, minerals and chemicals in biological processes, and water's surface tension enables our body to mobilize these elements efficiently.

—Up to 60 percent of the human body is water, the brain is 75 percent water, blood is 82 percent water, and lungs are nearly 90 percent water.

—The body loses water via the skin by perspiration, kidneys by urine, lungs by exhaled water vapor, and intestine by feces.

—At normal activity levels, people lose two to three cups of water a day in perspiration. But during an hour of vigorous exercise, people sweat out approximately a quart of water. Deep yellow or amber colored urine can be a sign of dehydration.

With all that in mind, here are five tips for maintaining proper hydration.

—Don't wait until you're thirsty to drink water. By the time you feel thirsty, you probably have already lost two or more cups of your total body water.

—Don't substitute caffeinated coffees, teas, sodas or alcoholic beverages for water. Caffeine and alcohol can act as diuretics, causing you to lose water through increased urination.

—Don't underestimate the amount of fluids lost from perspiration. You need to drink two cups of water for each pound lost following a workout.

—Start and end your day with a serving of water. Your body loses water while you sleep.

—When it's warm outside, cold water is the best fluid for keeping hydrated. Cool water is absorbed much more quickly than warm fluids and may have a positive effect on cooling off your overheated body."

If you are not sure you're drinking pure water in those amounts, keep a mental or, even better, a written log of your water intake for a few days. Gradually increase water as you gradually decrease the drinks that do not hydrate you (soft drinks, alcohol, and caffeinated drinks). You will be amazed once you get used to feeling better.

Think about your house plants or your garden: when you don't give a plant enough water, everyone agrees that it is stressed. Why not realize that your organs are stressed when not watered enough? If you live in North America, the odds are 3 to 1 that you are short on water, according to Dr. Levine, and therefore putting stress on every system of your body. Stress is not just emotional upset; it includes the taxing of the body outside its operating limits. Stress in your body makes surgery and recovery more difficult. Lowering stress makes surgery easier and recovery faster and more comfortable.

The human body, inactive, requires *at least* one ounce of water daily for every two pounds of body weight. Even the guidelines suggested above are limited because they do not take body weight and activity into account. If you weigh 150 pounds and do not exercise much, you can get by with 75 ounces of water per day. That's a little over nine 8-ounce glasses. If, on the other hand, you move your body or think of yourself as an active person, The International Sports Medicine Institute in Los Angeles suggests 2/3 ounce of water for every pound of body weight. At 150 pounds, that's 100 ounces of water. Not juice, beer, sodas, or any other beverage that requires the body to use energy to process and digest it.

Try to minimize the liquids that pull water out of you. Drinks with sugar require extra effort from your body. Artificial sweeteners are worse. There is no substitute for water. If two out of three North Americans are chronically dehydrated, which group are you in? Even inactive adults lose between five and six glasses (40-48 ounces) of water just from normal perspiring, urinating, and exhaling. That fluid needs to be replaced.

Inflammation and Hydration

Inflammation is a major source of post-surgical discomfort, otherwise known as pain. If you want to keep inflammation down, and I trust you do, you must understand that poor hydration promotes inflammation. You get the benefit of lowered inflammation by starting to increase water several days before you go in for a procedure. It doesn't do to wait until a nurse hydrates you with an IV. It's just not the same. Unless your doctor indicates otherwise because of your particular case, get used to increasing water intake. Yes, you will urinate more at first. It's healthy, normal and good for you, since you are flushing out toxins. Think of it as letting go of stress-causing stuff.

After a while, most of us don't urinate more often, but eliminate more volume each time, as our bladders get used to the idea of normal hydration. For example, I drink lots of water, am over 60, and never get up in the night. My body knows how to adjust. So does yours, most likely.

Check with your doctor to make sure more water is OK for you, especially if you have a kidney issue. There could be medical reasons important to your situation. When in doubt, follow your doctor's advice.

If you knew that the water in your body always responded with increased beauty to thoughts of love, appreciation, and gratitude, wouldn't you consider giving your water such thoughts again and again? Let me remind you of the pictures in Dr. Emoto's *Message from Water*, which I mentioned in an earlier chapter. Imagine the water in your body looking beautiful and harmonious as you think thoughts of love, appreciation, and gratitude. Take it one step further and know that you are having an effect: on other people, on animals, plants, on yourself, on anything containing water. Imagine, for fun, that you can make water more beautifully organized wherever you direct your attention and love. It's the least expensive way to restructure water.

Try this little practice at least once today: send energy through your hands to a glass or cup of water while saying a prayer or blessing of your choice. Notice how it feels. Why not? This is another no-risk strategy that, at the very least, puts positive energy into circulation. You can't go wrong.

CHAPTER 11
Protect Your Sleep

"O sleep! O gentle sleep!
Nature's soft nurse, how have I frighted thee,
That thou no more wilt weigh my eyelids down,
And steep my senses in forgetfulness?"
William Shakespeare, Henry IV, part 2

"And if tonight my soul may find her peace
in sleep, and sink in good oblivion,
and in the morning wake like a new-opened flower
then I have been dipped again in God, and new-created."
D.H. Lawrence

I use the word *sleep* so may times in this short chapter that you might think I'm trying to hypnotize you. Not really, but I do want you to know how important a subject we're dealing with. You may discover good ideas here worth the price of the entire book. If the angels of sleep seem to have absented themselves from you for a while, you can help them return.

Sleep is the chief agent of healing. Your body and your mind repair themselves in sleep. The more you get before your operation, and after, the more likely you are to do well in surgery, and after, provided the quality is good. You are blessed if you sleep well. Your recovery will be faster than it would be if you did not. Do not despair, though, if you do not, for there are many things you can do. Just about everybody can improve the quality of their sleep by putting into practice even a few of the simple suggestions in this chapter. Quality is the major factor, not quantity.

First, let me give you a quick overview of the "normal" sleep cycle. It is useful to know how it works, and really pretty simple. The first 20 minutes or so after you nod off are Stages 1 and 2, entry levels, where the body performs metabolic tasks such as digesting food. Then comes deeper sleep, Stages 3 and 4, when the body carries out anabolic (building up) processes such as synthesizing proteins to repair cell walls, rebuilding bones, restocking immune cells and more. These deeper stages are when physical repair—of the skin, bones, tissue, and muscle—takes place. Ideally, there's about an hour of deep sleep in each sleep cycle, after which your body cycles back down, goes limp, and you enter REM, the stage where most dreams happen.

Sleep expert Dr. Eve Van Cauter, of the University of Chicago, tells us to think of REM as "psychological recuperation." She continues: "We seem to have a "primal need for the emotional tonic of dreams."1 Each entry into REM at the end of a cycle brings the sleeper close to awakening. Good sleepers drop back down, through the stages, into deep sleep after REM, but people who suffer from one of the forms of insomnia often wake up at this point and can't get back to sleep. This cycle of about two hours repeats 3-4 times a night when things are going well. High quality sleep involves all the stages in good proportion.

The custom in our culture is to get less deep sleep as we get older, but that does not mean that poor rest and restoration are inevitable as we age. Nor is it true that we need less as we get older, according to Dr. Van Cauter. We actually require the same amount throughout our lives, but unfortunately, many people over 45 in Western society do not sleep well or deeply.2 Accumulated habits play the biggest part in sleep loss, not the inevitability of biological aging. There are 80 year-olds who sleep very well, while teenagers and young adults are the worst sleepers of any age group in our society. You can sleep better than you do now, no matter how young or old you are. And you can have an improvement right away. Read on.

One of the benefits of deep sleep (Stages 3 and 4) is that the pituitary gland produces about 70% of its Human Growth Hormone (HGH) during these stages. The more deep sleep you get, the more natural HGH you produce. HGH production seems to decline with age. It appears that at least some of the decline is a function of less deep sleep, rather than biological aging. HGH is not well understood yet, but indications are that a natural increase in HGH production promotes self-healing, overall good body functioning and a slowing of the aging process.

One thing is certain: not getting enough Stages 3 and 4 sleep means the body is not repairing itself and is therefore declining abnormally rapidly and aging too fast. A note of caution: there are a number of vendors trying to sell us on the idea of taking HGH in pill form. This is not an effective strategy and possibly dangerous to your health. Consult your doctor before taking any hormone directly. Naturally induced deep sleep is the best remedy. The last part of this chapter contains suggestions of how to get what you need.

Americans spend over $500 million per year on sleep medications, many of which zonk you into Stages 1 and 2, while minimizing deep sleep. You might be among those who feel grateful for just being able to go unconscious at night and may not object to this, but in the long run, we all require the deeper stages. Some sleep is definitely better than none, but the fact remains that body restoration takes place only in deep sleep. Without it, restoration is slowed and the aging process is accelerated. If you are being prescribed a sleep medication, ask your doctor what is known about its effect on the deep stages. Medication for sleep is almost always unhealthy in the long run.

Your body, mind and spirit are absolute in requiring the best rest you can get. Quality is the key, not time spent in bed. If you are putting some of the material in other chapters of this book into practice, you will reduce stress naturally and your body will surely need less medication to sleep well. Natural stress reduction is much better for you than chemicals. The best advice is to use pharmaceutical sleep medication only in desperate circumstances on a limited basis. Remember to bring your doctor a written list of all medications you are taking, Ask your doctor if they interfere with your sleep cycle. If they do, is there a change of medication or a natural remedy that might work?

A minor point that some people are curious about: researchers at Oregon Health Sciences University found that melatonin, once thought of as the insomniac's miracle, brings on mostly light sleep while reducing the deep (Stages 3 and 4) sleep so vital for physical repair.3 Extremely small doses might have some benefit. Ask your doctor. Melatonin has, however, been used effectively to reset the body clock, either when it's been disrupted or when changing time zones. That's a one-shot deal, not for daily use. Keep in mind that melatonin is a hormone. If you are thinking of taking any hormone directly, which can be risky, seek competent medical advice.

What to Do: A Quick Summary of Known Sleep Tips

As with the entire book, choose the suggestions that work for you. All of these practices have helped people sleep better, but nothing fits everybody. Some are so simple they take no time at all. The idea is to choose something that feels possible, maybe two somethings, make a few small changes in routine and allow them to work, which in turn might encourage you to try a few more.

Aerobic exercise

Especially in the afternoon or evening. Participants in one study, all over the age of 67, were divided into two groups. One group did stretching exercises; the other did aerobic exercise three times a week for 45 minutes in the late afternoon. The aerobics group participants got 33% more deep sleep than they did before the study began, and produced 30% more Human Growth Hormone. No one in the stretching group increased sleep or HGH levels. The conclusion is that producing heat in your body is effective. Afternoon exercise, especially, raises body temperature slightly until bedtime, which in turn helps the body fall into deeper sleep.

A hot bath

A bath an hour or two before bed brought about more deep sleep in one study. The hotter the better, up to 105 degrees, the report says. Lukewarm didn't work as well. Just before you get in, take a cup or so of Epsom salts and drop into it any of these essential oils, singly or in any combination: *Lavender, Bergamot* and *Frankincense*, up to 10 drops total. The Epsom salts help with dispersal, so your body doesn't get all the oils in one spot. Pour the mix into the bath. Breathe well. If you have no bath, take a hot shower and put a drop each of Lavender, and one of the others, on a washcloth or tissue and breathe it in, or use one of the methods described in more detail in Chapter 13.

Relax

Give the techniques in this book a workout. Try the Relaxation Response, the breathing exercises, prayer, guided recordings, or your own method. The idea is to slow down your whole system and remove stress all day – and especially before bedtime. Combine a breathing routine with a bath. You might try this simple rhythm: breathe in to a count of four, and let your breath release freely to a count of eight. Repeat 20 times.

Make love
With caring, tenderness, and equal exchange of pleasure, it works well to aid good sleep. If you have no partner, love yourself. No guilt. It's good for you.

Go to bed at a regular time
Even more useful, make an effort to reduce some of the many forms of stimulation we all have around us. A good start would be to avoid alcohol and caffeine for 3-4 hours before bedtime. Television is ridiculously stimulating, especially the news, violent material, and commercials. Turning off the TV at night can make a noticeable difference. Start to turn the lights down a little earlier. On the subject of stress reduction, can you imagine some way to agree with your family to have intense discussions—I mean arguments, fights and potentially stressful discussions—before dark, or not at all, until you are recovered? And after.

Natural teas
Have a nice cup of chamomile tea or one of the good herbal sleep teas in the evening (Celestial Seasons has one called "Sleepy Time").

A pinch of salt
A pinch on your tongue at bedtime followed by a small glass of water (4-6 ounces). An old folk remedy

Hear stress-lowering, peaceful music
Go to the next chapter for suggestions. Listen by candlelight, by the fire or in the bath. Make your own music. Add essential oils.

Toning
Hum or sing to yourself. Toning has many benefits, one of which is facilitating sleep through stress reduction. Instructions are in the next chapter.

Listen to a good hypnosis or guided imagery tape or CD
Choose one designed to bring deep sleep, or use your surgery preparation recordings. My favorite sleep tape is from Glenn Harold, from Diviniti Publishing in England. If you don't mind a strong non-U English accent, his sound work is fabulous, with cool multi-layered voice and sound moving around in your head. His voice, once you get into it, feels unusually caring. In our house, we know it works. See *Resources* for his and other recommended recordings.

Live hypnosis session

If sleep has been an ongoing issue for you, I suggest you find a good hypnotherapist and have a live session, usually more powerful than recordings—and it can be individualized.

Fresh air

Japanese sleep experts have discovered that Stage 3 and 4 sleep is maximized when your head is 7-10 degrees cooler than the rest of your body. That's why they make special pillows that draw heat away from your head. Open a window. Maybe take a short walk outside before bed. Walk the dog, even if you don't have one.

No light at night

If you have to get up in the middle of the night, do not turn on the light. Sleep research shows that light in the middle of a sleep cycle throws off the biological clock for 3-4 days. The light brings an immediate lag to the body clock, delaying the release of hormones and sleep processes by an hour and a half or more. For a person needing more sleep right now, stress is added. The sleep loss goes on for several days.4 Many illnesses are currently being linked to disruption of the body's circadian rhythm. If you need light to get up in the night, do what the US Army does for its soldiers before night activity: use a dim red light. Put red cellophane over a flashlight near your bed.

Use a sleep mask

Even a little light, from a streetlight outside or a nightlight, for example, can alter the quality of sleep. I use a sleep mask from Nikken that puts out a slight magnetic field around the eyes and pineal gland (where natural melatonin comes from). I found out how much I liked it one winter night when I was safely tucked in bed. I realized I had taken it to the living room to show someone and forgotten it. Yes, I got out of bed. I love it. Yours doesn't have to be magnetic, just so it keeps light out. This item is a must for your hospital kit if you're going to stay overnight.

Supplements

Calcium and Magnesium after supper act to comfort and relax. Our bodies take in these minerals best during sleep. I use a Calcium-Magnesium formula which also contains small amounts of Valerian Root, Hops, and Chamomile, which all nudge the body to relax a bit more. Some people do well with Vitamin B3, also known as Niacin, taken after supper. Start with a tiny amount and increase slowly until you get a mild reaction. Too much makes most people heat up and become rather flushed, which you may find uncomfortable for a few minutes. Drinking more water will make this go away soon, but I prefer to have a gentle warming on a small dose.

Lecithin helps bring on restful sleep. Two to four tablespoons of powder, found at health food stores, is a good amount. Lecithin is also found in eggs and soy products. It is a harmless and helpful nutritional supplement.

Seafood, chicken, milk, cheese, yogurt, cashews and watermelon all contain the amino acid L-tryptophan. It is one of the amino acids that your body uses to make neurotransmitters, such as serotonin. Neurotransmitters are chemical nerve messengers that help your brain to shut down for the night and be fully awake during the day. More of the L-tryptophan in dairy products gets to your brain when you have a carbohydrate along with it. That's why cheese and crackers, or milk and a whole-grain cookie are good hour-before-bedtime snacks.

One of the best things about natural sleep aids is that they are safe and not habit forming. When your brain and body are well nourished, more restful sleep is a natural result. You are feeding your body, not drugging it.5

There's one more thing I just can't leave out. I recently came upon a very interesting CD, titled *BioRecharge*. The producers state that a user can increase natural deep sleep and HGH production by listening, through headphones, to specially designed sounds when going to sleep. I don't know if that claim is true or not. Nevertheless, I couldn't resist trying it and have played it about 40 times. I have noticed being better rested after going to sleep with this recording. It feels good to me. The text on the CD cover says this about the 35 minute track called *"The Body Rejuvenator:"*

"Specific window frequencies targeted for release of Human Growth Hormone. These frequencies also induce very profound delta states, the deepest level of rest the mind obtains during Stage 4 sleep." The CD also contains two other tracks of designed sounds and frequencies: *"Fog Buster"* and *"Mental Sharpener."* Part of the purpose of the recording is to enable people to use less medication. It should not be surprising that sounds can affect brainwaves. A lot of information is flowing around right now about sound and vibration healing. See Chapter 12 for more.

In The Hospital

This is where your sleep mask and earplugs really come in handy. There are always sounds and lights in a hospital. You can block some of them with mask and plugs.

The other big challenge is night awakenings for medication or tests, or some other nonsense. Ask your doctor about working out how to get more uninterrupted sleep. Doctors are becoming more aware that sleep is their ally, so you have reason to expect a good response.

Use your tape player and headphones to listen to sleep tapes and relaxing music. It helps keep the hospital sounds out. Use the *Cocoon of Light* exercise from Chapter 7 to feel safe and secure.

A Last Note

My sincerest wish for you is that you sleep well and pharmacy-free, for natural deep sleep is your greatest and most powerful healing ally. It builds your strength and supports your recovery. I have little doubt that one or more of the above suggestions will work. All you have to do is…something.

CHAPTER 12
Music for Recovery

"Take a music bath once or twice a week for a few seasons, and you will find that it is to the soul what the water bath is to the body."
Oliver Wendell Holmes

"A man should hear a little music, read a little poetry, and see a fine picture every day of his life, in order that worldly cares may not obliterate the sense of the beautiful which God has implanted in the human soul."
Johann Wolfgang von Goethe

Why Music? Listening to music before, during and after your procedure can enhance your experience more than you might guess. In *The Mozart Effect*, a great book about the myriad therapeutic effects of music, Don Campbell says: "By listening to music with longer, slower sounds, one can usually deepen and slow the breath, allowing the mind to calm down. As with breathing rates, a lower heartbeat creates less physical tension and stress, calms the mind, and helps the body heal itself. Music is a natural peacemaker."1

You can also use music to create states of relaxation, enhanced learning, concentration and more. Healing with sound is as old as humanity. Shamans have been chanting over sick patients for countless thousands of years. In Greece, Pythagoras used special songs and incantations with particular melodies and rhythms, to cure diseases of the body and mind. The Asclepions, or healing temples, in Greece used music as one of the primary healing modes. Music is a form of nutrition: consider it as food for our non-physical, or subtle, bodies.

Sound healing means the therapeutic application of sound frequencies to the body-mind of a person with the intention of bringing them into a state of harmony and health. The French ear, nose and throat specialist Dr Alfred Tomatis has devoted the last 50 years to understanding the ear and its function. He believes that the ear is the most important of all our sense organs. The ear controls the body's sense of balance, rhythm and movement and is the conductor of the entire nervous system. Through the medulla, the auditory nerve connects with all the muscles of the body. Hence, muscle tone, equilibrium, flexibility and vision are affected by sound. Through the vagus nerve, the inner ear connects with the larynx, heart, lungs, stomach, liver, bladder, kidneys, small intestine and large intestine. Every organ, every bone and every cell in the body has its own resonant frequency. Together they make up a composite frequency like the instruments of an orchestra. When one organ in the body is out of tune, the whole body is affected. With sound, it may be possible to bring a diseased organ into harmony with the rest of the body, Tomatis maintains. For more information about Tomatis and his work, visit the official website: www.tomatis-group.com

The studies are consistent in their findings: the right kind of music reduces anxiety and reduces the experience of pain, and therefore the need for pain medication. In one study, patients hearing healing music had half the amount of postoperative anxiety and used half as much painkiller, 21% less in another type of surgery.[2] Results vary from person to person, but the right sounds are likely to help. Music has been found to decrease the need for anesthesia: patients had excellent comfort with smaller-than-usual doses of pain medications. If you have less anesthesia and other meds in you, your body recovers more easily.[3] In a nutshell, patients have a more pleasant experience all around when they listen to music, and leave the hospital sooner. What could be better? It's harmless, cheap, non-fattening, and does you good.

One of the best artists in the specialized field of music healing, Dean Evenson (see below for his recordings), adds this comment:

"Sound affects the vibratory rate of every cell and molecule in the body and has a direct impact on the muscles, nervous system, digestive system and circulatory system. It is no wonder that both mainstream and alternative health care practitioners are using music like "Sound Healing" (the title of one of his CDs) either alone or in combination with traditional medical practices as a support in the healing process."[4]

Just for fun, here's some academic-medical language in support:

"Music therapy complements conventional medicine to effect changes in behavior, emotions, and physiology and to reduce psychophysiologic stress, pain, anxiety, and isolation."[5]

And one more:

"By providing a comforting auditory milieu, intraoperative music may decrease patient anxiety and consequently minimize patient-controlled conscious sedation and analgesic requirements. In two randomized controlled trials, patients who listened to favorable music required significantly less propofol for sedation with spinal anesthesia (P [is less than] .001) and had significantly less alfentanil requirements during lithotripsy."[6]

Intraoperative means during the operation, in case you were wondering. You don't want to know what lithotripsy is unless you're having one. The P numbers refer to the probability of the results occurring by chance. P=.001 would mean the likelihood is one in a thousand. The medical profession is learning now about the power of good music to help you recover.

In a study done in 1999 under the auspices of National Institutes of Health, one group of patients listened to their choices of harp, piano, synthesizer, symphonic or slow jazz and did a relaxation exercise. A control group used pain medication. The researchers found that "relaxation and music, separately or together, significantly reduce patients' pain following major abdominal surgery." The leader of the study concluded: "Both medication and self-care methods which involve patient participation are needed for relief. These relaxation and music self-care methods provide more complete relief without the undesired side effects of some pain medications...Patients can take more control of their postoperative pain using these self-care methods. Nurses and physicians preparing patients for surgery and caring for them afterwards should encourage patients to use relaxation and music to enhance the effectiveness of pain medication and hasten recovery."[7]

The same article makes a major point about the significance of pain reduction:

"The findings have important implications for the 23 million people who undergo surgery and experience postoperative pain annually in the United States. Pain can hamper recovery by heightening the body's response to the stress of surgery and increasing tissue breakdown, coagulation and fluid retention. Pain also interferes with appetite and sleep and can lead to complications that prolong hospitalization."

Pain itself can slow healing, as can too many chemicals. The middle way is a sincere effort at self-help to minimize the medications. A news release from the University of Buffalo Medical School sheds further light from a slightly different angle:

"Older adults who listened to their choice of music during outpatient eye surgery had significantly lower heart rate, blood pressure and cardiac work load than patients who did not listen to music…Furthermore, the music-listeners rated themselves significantly less anxious and significantly better at coping with the experience than their non-music-listening colleagues."8

It's just that simple. Find music you like that relaxes you. Not fast, not syncopated, not loud, not heavy, not stimulating. If you haven't got one already, buy a small CD player or cassette player with headphones. You'll find yourself listening more.

One other key bit of data from the Buffalo study tells us something important about outpatient surgery. Heart rate and blood pressure of all patients (all of them over 55) shot up the morning of surgery, indicating that outpatient surgery may be more stressful than commonly believed. The stress indicators for this so-called "minor" surgery were at pretty much the same levels as for patients having "major" inpatient operations. These measures of cardiovascular stress dropped significantly in the music-listening group within 10 minutes and remained low. Only in the music group did cardiovascular measures nearly reach baseline.

Why not start relaxing with music right now? Give yourself a time for relaxation, when you say your healing statements or play with imagination exercises, or just relax and sink into the sounds. I especially recommend it if you're usually too busy to take time for yourself. Listen to your hypnosis or guided imagery recordings during your personal time. The more you use the tools to relax, the easier it gets, because relaxation is a skill you easily learn with practice. Keep in mind that lowering stress leads to optimal outcomes. If healing music only lowered stress, it would be worth having, but it does so much more.

Toning

Before I talk about what kind of listening music seems to work best for your needs, I'd like to put in a word for the practice of toning. Toning is defined as using the voice to make a long sound with an elongated vowel, on one note. When you make any sound, the vibrations reverberate throughout your body, touching every part. When you put a little oomph, plus intention, into a sound you make, it penetrates into every cell. Think of toning as an amazing tool for self-healing. It costs nothing, heightens body awareness, and puts you in touch with a sense of control of how you feel. Even if you believe you can't sing, you can still make a long sound. It makes no difference whether it sounds "good" or not. Give it a try.

Find yourself a place you can experiment where you won't feel self-conscious. Take a comfortably deep breath into your diaphragm. Let it out slowly, making a long "Aaah" from your diaphragm. That's it. You're toning already. Make another sound, on a lower note, and be aware of where it vibrates inside you, Make a higher sound and feel where it's located. Sing it. Try any vowel sound in various notes, feeling the sound wherever it is in your body. If you play with it while taking walks, or in the shower, you'll probably find you can move the vibrations all around, even into tense areas. Be daring: add a consonant. Om. Rah. La, whatever sounds right to you.

Regular toning and humming help to re-energize the physical body and restore health to all your subtle bodies. Toning boosts the immune system and brings about the release of endorphins, which act as natural pain relievers. Toning assists in good breathing and posture. Regular toning massages and stimulates the muscles of the digestive system. It can help insomniacs—and others—find sleep.

Toning with other people creates a feeling of unity. That's why people get together and chant 'Om" or other sounds. Everybody feels better. Practice toning in a healing circle with your Support Team. Try it and see. Have fun and feel good.

For more information about toning, check out Don Campbell's work. He has a tape that explains and instructs and has a wonderful website with a lot of good information. Joy Gardner-Gordon's book, *The Healing Voice,* has lots of good stories and information on healing with toning. See *Resources,* Appendix C.

What Music?

The research shows that the music that works best for our purpose is harmonious, even-tempered, with no surprises and no words. The studies call it *anxiolytic* music, which means non-anxiety-producing.9 Naturally, a lot of music that we like to listen to for pleasure includes tension. Normally, that's fine. But think of music as food for your nervous system. As with food for eating, when you're strong and healthy, your body can make use of an array of tastes. When you're not at your best, it is wise to feed yourself what does you good right now and avoid what doesn't.

The research doesn't favor a lot of music we might normally listen to, whether symphonies, rock music, or even 40s ballads. Most music contains tension and suspense on purpose, to keep our interest level high. Favorite rhythms might speed up body functions that need to be slowed down just now. Familiar music can also evoke many memories and associations, stimulating the brain to work in pathways that may not support fast recovery. Songs with lyrics are not advised, similarly, because they might bring up specific memories and feelings.

The best material is beautiful and dreamy. Fast rhythms, which speed up heartbeat, are not recommended. Getting stimulated or excited is not what you need, especially not during your procedure, or as the doctors would say, intraoperatively. When you're feeling strong, well into recovery, your favorite stimulating music is great.

Just for now, do your best to avoid unsettling sounds. Heavy metal, punk and rap seem to be the strongest opponents of your healing system. Syncopated beats are the wrong kind of stimulation. They excite the heart, organs, and blood way too much. Your body will tell you what's good for it, provided you allow it to. Does the music encourage taking longer, slower breaths? Does it make you feel as if you could relax into a comfortable position, feeling safe and secure? If it doesn't, do yourself a favor and let it go for now.

Early classical music (Bach and Monteverdi, especially) seems to work well, provided the selections are not too fast or exciting. Bach's *Goldberg Variations* made lovely crystals of Emoto's water, perhaps, as he writes, because the composition was intended as a gift of gratitude and appreciation, which the music seems to transmit. In the days preceding your operation, it works best to keep the music calm and reflective. The point is to keep excitement down as much as possible. In this vein, I especially like the work of a British ensemble, Sulis Music. They are classical musicians who specialize in healing sounds.

There are excellent tapes and CDs specifically designed to help with the healing response. Several titles that seem to work well are listed just below. It is not a complete list, by any means, so if you know of compositions you like better, use them. Let me know, by way of my web site, what you like and I'll post the suggestions. Choose one or two or several. You can't go wrong with any of these. All of them slow down heart rate and breathing, bringing you deep relaxation.

Belleruth Naparstek's *Successful Surgery* set, already a must-have, includes a long piece suitable for play during a procedure or for relaxation any time. I suggest you have a few other selections, for before and after your operation, to keep your interest up.

When you go in for your procedure, have your player and headphones and chosen recordings. Use them from the moment you sit down in the waiting room (or wherever you are first placed), and any time you find yourself waiting in a holding area or corridor. If your surgeon allows, listen during the procedure, while in the anesthetic state; and after, when you're recovering. It really helps having the sounds for those in-between moments when you need a comforting influence. If you have time, consider listening to your hypnosis or imagery recording. Keep in mind that you can get help from a nurse or your anesthesiologist to keep your music going. Ask.

It is now well established that patients hear everything while in the anesthetic state, even if we don't consciously remember. Having your own music helps mask the sounds around you and allows you to use every sound, even the voices of the surgical team, to go deeper into relaxation.

Recommended Recordings

—Sulis Music: One of the loveliest albums to be found anywhere. A real find for the soul in search of well-designed healing music. This group of healer-scholar-musicians has its roots in early classical. Here is real food for the inner being.

—Dean Evenson: *Forest Rain*. Nature sounds, rain, flute, other instruments. Very relaxing. Also good for a peaceful work environment.

The Tao of Healing. Evenson's flute with Professor Li Xiangting, who plays the guqin, an ancient Chinese seven-string zither. Great recording. I can listen to this often. Also *Sound Healing.*

—Riley Lee: *Yoga Tranquility, Buddha's Dream, Sanctuary: Music From A Zen Garden*

Riley Lee is a shakuhachi master. The sounds are spacious, lovely, thoughtful, and easy to take. These recordings are exquisite. You can't go wrong.

—Stan Richardson: *Shakuhachi Meditation Music.* (2 tape set)

Richardson is also great. I feel encouraged to go calm and deep with this album.

—David Darling:: *Eight String Religion.* Mellow cello and other good sounds.

—Stephen Halpern: *Accelerating Self-Healing.* This title speaks for itself.

—Jonathan Goldman: *The Lost Chord.* Mantras, overtones, and chants from the Hindu, Tibetan and Hebrew traditions. Mysterious stuff also, such as "psychoacoustic frequencies and sound ratios." Also *Holy Harmony.* Sacred chants and tuning forks. The tones help the body organize for self-healing. This is great material.

—Abbess Hildegard of Bingen: *A Feather on the Breath of God.*

One of my all-time favorites. Beautiful, spacious, long-breath, meditative female voices. Hildegard possessed, in the 12th century, a profound grasp of the effects of music on the soul

—Gregorian Chant: *Lost in Meditation* Volume I and/or Volume II

Beautiful, expansive, comforting, soul-enhancing Gregorian chants. Exquisite male voices. What more can I say? These excellent albums are less than $6.00 each at amazon.

—Monroe Hemi-Sync   *Pain Control* (verbal), Masterworks

I've added this recording because the Monroe hemi-sync process is helpful at balancing left and right hemispheres of the brain. Users have found this recording effective for transcending short or medium duration pain at a low cost.

—Chuck Wild, Liquid Mind: *Slow World*

Unobtrusive, peaceful, uplifting. Great tape. I find myself playing this a lot.

There are lots of others, but three or four of the above should give you a good start. The point of the sound healing recordings is that they help our body do what it wants to do naturally: quicker self-repair, pain relief, stress reduction, and increased well-being. Links to these and others are in the *Resources* section of my website.

CHAPTER 13
A Hint of Aromatherapy

> "If the day and the night are such that you greet them with joy, and life emits a fragrance like flowers and sweet-scented herbs, more elastic, more starry, more immortal—that is your success."
> Henry David Thoreau (1817-1862)

Higher Body Nutrition

If we accept the notion that we have mental, emotional and spiritual bodies, as well as physical, it is not a far reach to accept that we require nutrition for these "higher being-bodies." If we don't have sufficient mental foods, for example, our mental lives show the consequences: we get dumber. If we don't take in spiritual nutrition, our spirits are at risk of diminishing. In the preceding chapter, I offered the suggestion that music is a subtle form of food. Entertain, if you will, the possibility that every sound, every smell, every sight, is a kind of food for one or more of those "bodies." OK. Maybe they aren't really bodies as we are accustomed to thinking of bodies. Let's just describe them as such for convenience.

You know that vibrations in the form of sound waves influence your state of mind. When you receive the stimulus of sound, your system has to digest it, which it does in a manner analogous to digestion of physical food. In a similar way, aromas function as food for the higher bodies. Your nose provides a direct channel to your brain, more direct than any other sense. Smells generate vibratory frequencies, which elicit emotional response. They trigger memories, thoughts, just about anything in your brain that can be stimulated. This passage, from Suzanne Fischer-Rizzi's *Complete Aromatherapy Handbook*, describes what happens when a scent hits the olfactory bulb and its complex and miraculous membrane:

"This olfactory membrane is the only place on the human body where the central nervous system is exposed and in direct contact with the environment. The cells of the olfactory membrane are brain cells. The hairs attached to the nerve cells—up to 80 million of them—are capable of carrying an incomprehensible amount of information, a capability that outperforms every known analytical function. With every breath we take, we receive the most minute pieces of information from our environment—with every breath we 'smell'"1

All smells, including essential oil aromas, are routed directly to the limbic brain, the most ancient part, without passing the cerebral cortex. Our subconscious receives and reacts to an aroma stimulus before we are conscious of it. Fischer-Rizzi explains: "Odor stimuli in the limbic system, or olfactory brain, release neurotransmitters—among them encephaline, endorphins, serotonin, and noradrenaline. Encephaline reduces pain, produces pleasant, euphoric, sensations, and creates a feeling of well-being. Endorphins also reduce pain, stimulate sexual feelings, and produce a sense of well-being. Serotonin helps relax and calm."2

That's just the beginning of the wonderful universe of possibilities in aromas. This brief chapter is only an introduction to a fascinating subject that is sure to become much more important. The reason for its emerging importance? Certain essential oils have been found to be fatally hostile to bacteria and viruses that have begun to resist antibiotics, particularly those commonly found in hospitals. These antibiotic-resistant strains are arousing profound concern in the medical community. Yet those same germs do not and cannot create resistance to the essential oils.

Right now, aromatherapy is probably your single best immediate defense against infection. Essential oils are capable of protecting you against a wide array of the germs in hospitals and everywhere else as well. But germ fighting is not the only benefit, for essential oils have powerful beneficial mood-altering and immune-enhancing capabilities as well.

Aromatherapy for Power Healing and Protection

Aromatherapy employs the essential oils of particular plants to alter mind-body states. The response has been observed for thousands of years. It is an ancient art, nearly as old as the use of sound in the healing process. Ancient peoples did not need double blind studies to tell them that the scent of lavender was calming, or what response they felt from the aromas released by burning or pressing certain plants. The power of scent is part of an almost-forgotten language of healing, now becoming known again as we collectively realize that modern medicine needs help from its ancient and wise cousins.

A recent newspaper article reports that MRI technologists at Irvine Regional Hospital are using drops of lavender, or sometimes cucumber, oil, in conjunction with music heard through headphones, to relax patients before they go through an MRI. The technologists report that this combined strategy reduces the stress of this noisy and sometimes scary procedure significantly.3 Medical people, especially nurses and technologists, are discovering the extent to which essential oil aromas can help patients. Naturally, having patients calm and relaxed makes their work happier and easier. The use of scents for peace of mind is spreading fast because it works in practice—and everyone can see it working.

Clinical studies have found essential oils to have therapeutic effects on psychological states such as depression and anxiety.4 Scents of several essential oils have been found to exert a therapeutic effect on brain waves and can encourage the healing process through relaxation and the relief of stress. A drop of lavender on a surgical mask, for example, provides a therapeutic aroma that can offset unpleasant odors and relieve anxiety before an operation.5

Practical Methods of Use

I'll repeat one very important point: certain essential oils have been found to be especially hostile to the survival of germs commonly found in hospitals. They work both inside the body and in the air. Specific instructions for taking practical advantage of this data are just ahead.

In addition, carefully chosen essential oils can elevate mood, lower stress and reduce physical or emotional discomfort. Several aromas seem most appropriate for you to use in the days before an operation, to bring about more calm optimism. Another group is good for in-hospital germ fighting. Several others seem just right for healing afterwards. Specific directions follow in a moment. Essential oils are safe, easy tools to use. If you know someone with knowledge, open a conversation. Maybe she or he will bring just the right thing into your life. There is so much possible through this mysterious and powerful healing art.

Now, here are the basic methods we have used. They have always been safe. The only consideration is that some people are sensitive to direct skin application of certain oils. In that case, we use unscented carrying oil, such as wheat germ, sesame, coconut or jojoba.

Foot Massage

Mix one or two drops of the recommended essential oil in a carrying oil or unscented massage oil, just enough to make a tiny puddle in the palm of your hand. Then massage it into the soles of the feet, where nerve endings communicate with your whole body. Or massage it into any place that feels good. The essential oil will penetrate through the skin and do its work. Get it on there 3-4 times a day. If no friend or helper is there, and you are able, apply it yourself. If you can't reach your feet, your hands and thighs will work. The beneficial properties are absorbed through the skin. Even though it's called aromatherapy, there is no need to inhale the scent for it to benefit you, although it can be quite pleasant. A whole body massage is even better, if you can get one.

Inhalation

Put a few drops of one or more oils on a tissue, let it dry a few seconds, and wave it gently under your nose.

Own a diffuser made for the purpose. I like simple ones with a candle under a dish of water into which you put a few drops of essential oil.

Spray

Use an atomizer bottle. We buy little blue or green spray bottles that make a fine spray. Put two or three drops of essential oil in filtered water. Mist it over your head, on your hands, your sheets, magazines, bedside table.

In the bath

If your doctor allows you baths, put up to 10-12 drops of essential oils, singly or in the combinations recommended below, in the bath just before getting in. Twice the benefit – you breathe it in and you take it in through the skin. A good method is to drip the oils first into a cup of Epsom salts, to help disperse them effectively and then pour the mix into the bath.

Which Essential Oils to Use

One of the best sources of information and excellent oils is a company called Young Living Essential Oils. I don't know if they are the best in the world. I do know that they make high quality, readily obtainable products and publish lots of good information. The quality has proved reliable over many years. You probably know an independent distributor. The other source I know and respect *is* Earth Essentials, available at many stores and less costly. We have used their products for years and get single oils from them. I get the combination formulas from Young Living. There may be other brands equally good, so if you know one, go ahead and work with it.

But some brands don't really provide the benefit. I have tried several store-bought aromas and have found several of them wanting in strength, longevity, and correct smell. The chief concern with essential oils is that too many companies adulterate their oils with synthetics or cheaper substitutes. If you know someone well versed in aromatherapy, ask for help and advice. With a knowing guide, aromas can be very powerful in affecting mind-body states. Although we have been using oils for years as a family, I consulted with my knowledgeable friend Jan Meredith, a generous Young Living distributor. The questions on my mind are: What has worked for people? What is simple enough so that people can do it with safety and ease?

Here are some of the essential oils and combinations that have been used with satisfaction by people we know. As before, these are options from which you choose what works for you. All the essential oils are safe and natural. They are a treat for the nervous system, not a treatment. If you have a friend who knows about oils, he or she may recommend different things altogether. Great. There are many other effective possibilities. I'm trying to keep my recommendations simple enough so that you won't be overwhelmed with too may possibilities. The following suggestions will definitely help, but they are not the whole story by any means.

Essential Oils in the Days before Surgery

The first goal is to help you strengthen your body's resistance to germs that could hurt you. Second, to help you increase internal energy. Third, to help you relax and be at ease.

Oregano *(Origanum vulgare ssp. Viride.)* The most powerful and consistent essential oil for making life difficult for infectious bacteria and viruses, according to recent research that tested more than 50 essential oils for efficacy against a number of germs.6 We put 2-3 drops in a carrying oil and massage it into the soles of the feet. It diffuses throughout the body. You might want to test a small area before applying it, as this oil can be a skin irritant when applied straight. Sometimes, we put 1-2 drops on a tissue, wait 10 seconds, and inhale. *Oregano* is best by itself; give it a few minutes with no other essential oils. Inhaled, it is traditionally said to enhance feelings of security and well-being. Use for days or weeks before surgery to build your internal germ resistance.

Frankincense *(Boswellia sacra).* A traditional support for the immune system, it relaxes and elevates the mind. It has been used from ancient times to ease and improve communion with the Creator. It is widely employed in hospitals in Europe. It has been considered a holy oil for perhaps 4000 years. Combine it freely with *Lavender* or layer one on top of the other.

Lavender *(Lavandula officinalis)* An all-purpose oil, it is used for calming, relaxing, and balancing, physically and emotionally. It is also used to speed wound healing and tissue regeneration, as a disinfectant, and to minimize scarring. Hostile to many pathogens that thrive in hospitals, it is one of the most versatile oils to have. Lavender is very helpful with burns. Folks with sensitive skin should mix lavender with carrying oil. We like the following methods:

Rubbing 1-2 drops of *Frankincense* or *Lavender* oil (or both) into the soles of our feet (or have a friend do it) 2-3 times a day.

Putting 1-2 drops, perhaps combined with *Frankincense*, in an atomizer to spray around our heads, or 1-2 drops on a tissue to inhale. These are both fine-smelling scents.

Taking a bath with one or both. Just when you are ready to step in the bath, add 3-4 drops of each mixed with Epsom salts. I love to add *Bergamot (Citrus aurantium ssp.bergamia)* as well. It is delicious. Traditional uses of these oils are relaxing the mind, stress reduction, and elevating the spirits. Your brain waves will be happy, especially if you combine the aromas with relaxation practice, healing music, or other strategies in this book. You might want to take one or more of the above with you to put on a tissue and inhale while you're waiting before surgery.

Valor ™: A formulation from Young Living, builds inner strength, a confident state of mind, and courage. It is intended to help empower the physical and spiritual bodies and is a great idea for building up inner strength. Contains *Spruce, Rosewood, Frankincense,* and *Blue Tansy*. Highly recommended.

In the Hospital

Any time your body is opened, some amount of trauma occurs. My first goal is to help you recover inner balance after the operation. Young Living's *TraumaLife*™ is the formulation of choice for this purpose. Originally designed for use in a project at several hospital trauma centers, it is especially grounding and calming after any shock to the system. It also helps with restlessness. It's the Mercedes of blends for recovery.

When we don't have it, we are pretty happy with the following excellent options for feeling better from the inside out:

—*Frankincense* and *Lavender* together—mixed or layered—on the soles of the feet with a little mixing oil if needed. Have a friend massage these oils anywhere you like. Another good combination is *Bergamot* and *Cypress (Cupressus sempervirens)*. *Bergamot* is traditionally helpful for alleviating worry, and is known to be inhospitable to respiratory and urinary tract infections, the two most likely types floating around the hospital.. *Cypress* helps bring a feeling of security, helps move fluids through the body for better healing and is unfriendly to many hospital germs. Any or all of these four oils combine well and smell really fine.

My second goal is to help strengthen your defenses against infection. Keep in mind that the biggest hazard in the hospital is picking up infection from the swarm of germs that can come to you through the air, on the hands of those treating you, on equipment, or settled on your bedside table and personal items.

For this purpose, we have used various combinations to improve immediate surroundings. I like spraying the air all around, which raises good feelings and makes life tough on airborne germs. *Oregano* remains at the top of the list for effectiveness and consistency.

Here's one formula that you might enjoy.

In a small atomizer or fine-spray bottle, mix the following with water:

2-3 drops **Lemon**
1-2 drops **Cinnamon Bark** *(Cinnamomum ceylanicum)* or *Lavender*
2 drops **Frankincense**

Lemon oil is a lifter of spirits, supports a clear mind, calms emotions, has good anti-bacterial properties, strengthens the immune system, clears airborne germs, and smells fresh and clear. *Cinnamon Bark* oil is second only to *Oregano* oil in creating a hostile reception for infectious bacteria and viruses. It's OK to omit the *Frankincense*, but nice to have it. *Bergamot* is good with this group, too. Any of these can be used alone. As an option, mix any combination of these, which all work well together:

2 drops **Eucalyptus Globulus**

2 drops **Lemon**

2 drops **Lavender**

2 drops **Frankincense**

Eucalyptus has very good germicidal properties. Suzanne Fischer-Rizzi says that a 2% solution evaporating in an aroma lamp will kill 70% of the staphylococcus bacteria in a room. It helps breathing, increases red blood cell activity and oxygen to all the cells in the body.7

I suggest continuing with some combination (personal tastes vary) from the above choices for the duration of a hospital stay. Friendly visitors (all part of your Support Team) can help keep you massaged, misted, or wafted. That's what friends are for.

Essential Oils to Use When You Go Home

Most of your healing takes place after you are discharged from hospital or surgery center. There are two areas to cover. First comes comfort and relief from discomfort. You can't go wrong with *Lavender, Lemon, Bergamot,* and *Frankincense,* massaged as indicated above. At home, you have the advantage of using an aroma lamp or ring to diffuse the scents. This is usually not OK in hospital, where other patients or staff might object. These oils are also likely to elevate your mood and create a good atmosphere for healing by subtly influencing your thoughts toward optimism, sort of an extra advantage.

Relieve It™, a special formulation from Young Living, is fabulous for tissue that remains sensitive. It contains *Hyssop, Spruce, Black Pepper, and Peppermint.* It works wonders to lower inflammation and relieve swollen tissue. It is usually applied, in a carrying oil, around the stitches (not in the incision) any time the bandaging is opened. These oils are enemies to germs, but don't run the risk of infection by rushing things. Work with your doctor.

PanAway ™, also from Young Living, has been good for us when there's a bone injury or trauma. We have used this after surgery that fixed a serious bone break. It makes it feel better.

Scar Management With Essential Oils

Once you are home, and the incision is sufficiently closed, here's a strategy for minimizing the scar as it heals: Alternate *Relieve It*™ with *Helichrysum* or *Frankincense* and *Lavender*. Apply as above, or use 2-3 drops of each, plus a pinch of sea salt, in a spray bottle that makes a fine mist. Spray this mix on the closed incision. If the incision is still open, wait.

Oil of *Helichrysum*, sometimes called *Immortelle*, is our primary helper as soon as it's OK to open the bandage. It helps relieve swollen tissue, relieves discomfort, and helps with reducing the scar. Since *Helichrysum* is expensive, you may substitute *Idaho Tansy*, which has many similar qualities, or use a combination of *Myrrh* and *Frankincense* oils. They are great for this purpose. Here's how to do it (This method applies to the formulas that follow, too.): Drip one drop onto the flat part of the end of your finger without touching the bottle to your skin. Rub the oil gently around the area of the incision, not in it. It doesn't take much. Add a drop at a time for a larger area.

A Strategy for Wound Healing Plus Scar Prevention:
24 drops **Lavender**
18 drops **Helichrysum** (or **Idaho Tansy**)
18 drops **Frankincense**

In 1-2 tablespoons of mixing oil. Apply once all around the incision, but not in it, 24 hours after the surgery. For continued scar minimization, keep the area oiled. Use your clean fingers to rub Vitamin E oil around the incision. Do this 3 times a day at least, for a week or more. Add a few drops of one of the above essential oils to the carrying oil. When the scar is a little farther along, simply use cold-pressed olive oil, almond or wheat germ oil to keep the area from getting dried out. This method is in common use among essential oil enthusiasts.

Dr Andrew Saul adds a note on Vitamin E: "Swelling around an incision can be greatly reduced by topical vitamin E dropped onto the suture line." He goes on to say: "Physicians and hospitals cannot rationally object to such use as long as you wait about five to seven days before application. This helps ensure that the wound has well begun to close." Used sooner, it could compromise the strength of the wound closure; Dr. Saul says that "topical vitamin E also reduces inflammation, itching, and that "pulling" feeling of a healing wound. Plus, it greatly reduces scarring."8 Check with your doctors to see if this is appropriate to your situation.

A Couple of Notes

Even though the essential oils are completely safe, get your doctor's OK if you wish to bring them into the hospital. Tell him or her what you want to do with them, just to be sure. If there is an objection, ask what the reason is. Does an essential oil truly interfere with treatment? Not likely, but listen to the reasons for the objection. Sometimes the nursing staff will try to take things away that you don't have written permission for. Your Support Team can be helpful by bringing you what you need and protecting you from busybody staff who might try to take it away.

Open air helps and speeds along incision healing, as long as you feel comfortable and safe. If you can, make an effort to get just a few minutes of sunshine on the incision as soon as you safely can, unless your doctor tells you not to. But only a few minutes. It's helpful, though, to take in a somewhat greater measure of sunshine with the rest of your body.

You can do a lot with a small effort by adopting one or more of these strategies. And, since hospitals are getting more and more used to using or allowing essential oils for healing, whatever you do might turn out not to be surprising to the staff. Nurses are showing lots of interest these days. I recommend getting help from your Support Team to assemble the essential oils, the carrying oil, and the mister. Either take them with you or have a friend bring them.

CHAPTER 14
Amazing Tools for Superior Healing

"A healthy soul stands united with the Just and the True, as the magnet arranges itself with the pole, so that he stands to all beholders like a transparent object betwixt them and the sun, and whoso journeys towards the sun, journeys towards that person."

Ralph Waldo Emerson, "Character"

Magnetic and Waveform Wellness Technologies
You have probably heard of the use of magnetic technologies in connection with various health issues. Japanese scientists and medical researchers have been studying the effects of static magnetic fields on the human body for over 50 years. More recently, they have been fascinated with the effects of far-infrared waves. Millions of people all over the world are using these two technologies to feel better.

I'll begin with far-infrared waves. They are generated by a special material, invented in Japan, that has been worked into everyday items such as comforters, socks, and sports wraps, even into long john underwear. These are waves that penetrate inches deep in the human body. They warm you from the inside out until you're just warm enough but not too hot. It's good magic. Good feelings happen for people who surround themselves with this wonder fiber. Being inside a far-infrared comforter is a fabulous feeling.

In our circle, we make sure anyone going to the hospital, or going in for an outpatient procedure, has, at the very least, a far-infrared Travel Comforter. We have sometimes been able to arrange for it to be on the patient waiting on a gurney before surgery. Then a nurse stashes it for surgery and brings it back for the ride to the recovery area, and back to the patient room. This is the best way to stay comfortable: not too hot, not too cold. We like having the energy near us for recovery, too. It seems to bring a feeling of great security. One friend, an MD, had a liver transplant and kept his Travel Comforter over the incision all day and all night for 8 weeks. He did not want to be without it and swore that the far-infrared waves speeded his healing and helped with the organ adaptation.

The second of these miracle technologies, magnetics, has a long history of assisting the healing process, at least 20 centuries. The presence of the right kind of static magnetic field around the human body seems to support conditions favorable to the body repairing itself efficiently. I am not talking about electro-magnetic fields, a somewhat different animal. The body is helped to work and repair itself as it's meant to. I have seen lots of good things happen when people use these technologies before, during and after surgery, and I have interviewed surgeons and anesthesiologists who have witnessed positive experiences in surgical patients. Doctors and patients report improved comfort levels, good incision recovery, more comfort, fewer problems, speedier healing and more vitality in the patients after procedures, using the products I talk about here.

There have been many magnet studies and trials in Japan, Korea, Russia, and, more recently, the US. Scientists have documented improvements in many different areas, such as improved sleep, relief from short and long-term discomforts in every part of the body and wound healing. I don't want to go on and on about studies. If you are scientific and want evidence, there's a wealth of studies summarized at *www.5pillars.com*. One paper, from Baylor College of Medicine, is worth mentioning: it reviews 117 separate studies of magnetic therapy in rehabilitation and explains the mechanisms of the biological effects of magnetic fields.1 The research shows a wide array of favorable results in clinical settings. Just as important, the positive experiences of over 5 million people in the US, Europe, and Asia over the last 20 years show that people get a verifiable wellness advantage from using the specific tools discussed below.

One of the few US studies of postoperative use of magnets comes from the Journal of Plastic and Reconstructive Surgery. A double-blind study of wound healing after liposuction showed that patients with magnets placed over the operative region "had significant reductions in pain on postoperative days 1 through 7, in edema (swelling) on days 1 through

4, and in discoloration on days 1 through 3 when compared with the control group."2 The researchers concluded: "These results demonstrated that commercially available magnets have a positive influence on the postoperative healing process in suction lipectomy patients." I know of hundreds of patients with many types of surgeries who attest to similar results using magnets from Nikken, the only reliable source I know. Drug store or mass-market magnets, by the way, are almost always bogus attempts to exploit the findings about the real things.

The two technologies, magnetics and far-infrared, work together to support states in which the human body feels safer, more comfortable, and can more easily energize the self-healing power we all have.

I'll tell you how I came to love these two tools. A few years ago, I fell backwards out of my garden shed and snapped a bone in my foot. This happened about a week after we had gotten a small mattress pad and a comforter, some small magnetic disks, and a few far-infrared ankle wraps. My foot began throbbing painfully. Then I began to oscillate between sweating for a few minutes, which changed to shivering—freezing cold, then back to sweating, and so on. Not a good sign. The idea hit me to lie down on the magnetic pad and pull the far-infrared comforter over me. Within five minutes, the wild swings stopped. I felt calmer. In another five minutes, I was comfortable, feeling safe and secure. I knew I was in a wonderful energy field that had eased me into a feeling of safety and comfort. My first thought was that these items, whatever they were, ought to be in every emergency vehicle.

Since then, I have heard from surgery patients who say they felt better much sooner than they could have imagined, crediting the difference to these technologies. They may all be nuts or self-deluded, but after I heard the same kind of reports many times, it sunk in. Something really strong happened for me that caused me to pay attention and listen to others who felt they had been helped. As I mentioned in Chapter 11, I also talked to many people who slept well for the first time in years because of the magnetic sleep system (I am one of those). Others have found reduced discomfort from a variety of aches, both long and short term. I'm convinced, after seven years of experience, that the energies are for real and are highly useful to almost everybody, especially surgery patients.

Forward-looking surgeons are increasingly encouraging the

integration of helpful complementary methods because they have learned that their results will be better when patients are relatively comfortable and relaxed. Anything that helps a patient feel better makes the work of the doctors more likely to succeed. We know that surgeons are hearing about these energy products from their patients. More and more, we're hearing from the docs "Yes, I've heard good things about that stuff…I've seen it help."

What I Have Used

Here are specific suggestions based on my experience and the experience of several physicians.. One of these is good; two are better, three better yet. If you get only one thing, make it the Travel Comforter, my personal favorite product. My family has used all these items for several years. We believe they have made our lives more comfortable and healthier. It is worthwhile to negotiate with the surgeon in order to have maximum contact with the energies through the whole time in the hospital.

—**Travel Comforter.** Far-infrared comforter that covers most bodies, yet folds up neatly into a small pillow. I love this. It is good for the chills, the shakes, or just feeling out of balance. We find it to have a centering effect. Some surgeons will OK it under plastic on the operating table. If yours will allow it, go for it. It's deeply comforting and helps your body stay at a good temperature. It acts as a stress relief tool.

—**Travel Pad.** This has both magnetic and far-infrared technologies. It is a body-length thin pad for putting under the sheets when you travel and still want the right energy field. We have sometimes been able to have it under patients (under a plastic protector) during surgery with the approval of the surgeon. I don't count on having it during surgery—it's a bonus. Next best is to have it as soon as you get back to your room. Most people feel better in the presence of these energies and almost everyone sleeps better. With this slim pad under you and the Travel Comforter on top, you will feel better and more secure.

—**Mini or SuperMini Magnets.** These are circular silver dollar size magnetic pads that include a far-infrared component. They can be used directly on or near the operative site. I have seen and heard from many patients who have placed them on the incision line after it has stopped bleeding (not before, of course). We like the increased comfort they bring to the area, which seems to heal faster with all the types of surgery I have heard of, as indicated by the liposuction study. The improvement they bring to the wound healing process is pleasantly surprising.

—**Sleep Mask**. An excellent black sleep mask with magnets embedded in it. The magnetic field is helpful for relaxing your eyes, even your whole face. It keeps the light out, too. Excellent for daytime naps and for keeping ambient light out of your eyes at night. Any light can interfere with depth of sleep. I have used one for 4 years and find I sleep better with it.

—**Thermal Socks**. Keeping my feet warm is a high priority. If it is for you as well, consider far-infrared socks that radiate warmth into your feet. It works even if they are wet—a wonderful feature of the fiber. They are good any time you want warm feet, in the hospital and at home.

If these technologies intrigue you, visit the website listed in *Resources*. You'll find lots of information there. If you know a Nikken Wellness Consultant, contact him or her. In the past, you might have heard a friend or neighbor talking about the wonders of Nikken's technologies. Perhaps you had doubts. Now would be a good time to talk to your knowledgeable friend.

CHAPTER 15
Conclusion

"I have come to the conclusion that politics are too serious a matter to be left to the politicians."
Charles de Gaulle

Paraphrasing General de Gaulle, I have come to the conclusion that health is too serious a matter to be left to the doctors. More realistically, it's up to each of us to participate as much as possible in our own healing process. I have shown you some possibilities. Use what you can. If one thing feels good, try some more. I encourage you to enjoy a lifetime of exploring further. You can feel safe trying any of the suggestions you have found here. Every piece you put into action can help ease your way. You may find some of the practices useful for years of living well.

You will find more information in *Resources*. There is no question that you can make a difference in your health and happiness that can last beyond your immediate recovery. You possess truly powerful tools for keeping yourself well.

What if we actually can bring more of our powers and abilities into play? Here's what I can promise you without fear of contradiction: if you use the exercises and information in even three or four chapters, you will be accessing more of your powers than ever, including the significant abilities of your subconscious mind to affect your physical states and external conditions.

Why not take these practices and attitudes and adapt them into your everyday life? Breathe, relax and let abundant well-being come in. No doubt it will if you allow it. Use various tools to strengthen your healing system. We can all be healthier, happier and more consciously alive. We can always feel more vitality. There is no limit. How many of us can truthfully say: "I'm perfect now, I don't need any more life force, I don't need any more well-being?"

Form Support Teams for others facing difficult or trying circumstances. Gather and focus intentional healing energy for the benefit of yourself and others. Recognize yourself as a healer when you help someone in need.

I ask you to think of Complementary Wellness as an area of study and practice that is related to, but different from Medicine. Medicine is the job of hospitals, clinics, doctors, nurses, and technicians. Students come from all over the world for American medical training because they see so much value in its knowledge. It is done well here. But there is one drawback: modern medical practice has oriented itself around fixing you when you're sick or injured. When you get to "OK," you're done. That means you've gone about as far as you can go in the medical system. Patients in our system of medical care often hear from their doctors something to the effect of "That's all I can do for you." And maybe also: "You'll have to live with it." It's left to us to discover who or what will take us beyond OK. What about getting to "GREAT?"

SICK _____ OK _____ GREAT

Maybe there's more to life than OK. What if feeling GREAT is up to you? I'll say flatly that working on healing your subtle bodies can take you beyond the limits of medicine. You can use the material in this book to alter your subtle bodies and bring you long-lasting radiant health.

Help is available. If you have begun to pull together your Support Team, you know that already. Most people, when not under stress, are good-hearted and willing to help others when asked. You can find help by asking, in the outer world and the inner. Angels await your call. You may sometimes find them dwelling in human bodies. Your request evokes a response on many levels. You have more allies and teammates than you ever imagined. Millions of us have been learning about non-traditional pathways to aliveness for many years. Wherever I go, I see more and more non-medical people functioning as healing helpers. I see more people studying how to be well and how to keep their families well. We are meant to rely on each other, to begin to trust ourselves to know what is good and useful for us. It is up to us to learn to trust ourselves to know who to listen to when we have a problem or crisis.

As I said at the beginning, I have seen many friends become helpless when they have a medical problem. Often, they get flooded with suggestions from friends and family, each with a pet remedy. They are confused, so they reject everything, the good along with the misguided, because they can't tell them apart. Then they wind up listening only to the MDs, who become the anchors of certainty. In these moments, everyone loses, even the doctors, who find themselves with patients unable to bring much of their own self-healing power with them. This book is intended to be your anchor in the storm. These are actions you can do without fear. They will without a doubt make your medical experience better. Let me remind you once again: I strongly suggest you ask *at least* one friend to read this book and find some part she or he can help you with. Healing is a community activity. It works better when you don't try to go it alone.

Coaching

Our society has an empty space between doctors and patients. Doctors are rarely in a position to inform you about most of the material in this book. They can't tell you about getting yourself to a state that is beyond OK, because most of them do not have time, do not know or are (correctly) afraid of running afoul of conservative state practice boards. They are, of necessity, required to concentrate on what they do best. They are in very demanding jobs that require enormous amounts of time and study. No one can pay attention to everything, especially not when it is outside of the usual boundaries of practice. Even so, doctors can still benefit greatly from the addition of Complementary Wellness practices, for such practices can help patients get better faster and attain higher states of well-being. Realize that medicine itself is a subset of the field of health. It is not the whole field.

Since surgery and medications are the principal tools of allopathic medicine, what happens to the rest of the healing process? I believe we need to have more and more non-medical people learning and sharing responsible information about the rest of the possibilities. Since self-healing is what every living being does naturally, why don't we all learn how to help each other do it better? You have probably already learned enough from this book to be a major help to someone else going into surgery. Be a coach for them. Show them a few ways to relax and heal.

As you know, coached patients do better. You don't need to be a doctor to offer useful help.

A coach who has experience with the material in this book can show you how to get the most out of it by helping you choose what you want, encouraging you, by finding practical ways to smooth your path and by helping you gather other teammates. A coach can help you do what you would like do for yourself. Naturally, a coach is not a doctor, does not practice medicine, and does not diagnose or give medical advice. Coaching is about helping you put into practice the spirit builders you choose to do, and then helping you keep with it.

It is the job of each and every one of us to make our own personal treatment and lifestyle choices. If you want help in moving beyond OK, having a wellness coach and a Support Team can make a difference. Some of us make it our work to support others in this way, but any kind person can be helpful.

Your part is to care enough about yourself to act independently and to be willing to receive the love and support of your community. If you've gotten this far, I congratulate you. You have made the magnificent choice of acting on your own behalf. That is the essence of self-healing.

> "If there is righteousness in the heart, there will be beauty in the character. If there be beauty in the character, there will be harmony in the home. If there is harmony in the home, there will be order in the nation. When there is order in the nation, there will be peace in the world."
>
> Chinese Saying:

APPENDIX A
Questions to Ask the Doctors

A 1993 survey showed that the average patient at a pre-surgery interview asks fewer than four questions in a 15 minute interview, one of which is almost always "Will you validate my parking?" You would ask more questions buying a TV, so go for it, since it's your health on the line. Ask the questions you need to. This is a great way to have a healing relationship with your surgeon. Ask about parking at the reception desk.

This is your time to gather information and collect confidence-building reasons to believe that your operation is right for you and that it will go well and that you are in able, professional hands. It's a time to develop trust and rapport. Treat the doctors as skilled team members and allow them, with your respect but not subservience, to function at their best. Be brief and address your main points. Good doctors appreciate good patients who ask good questions and are able to provide the information the doctor needs (like what medications you are taking).

Asking good questions has positive effects on your outcome. For one, the doctors know you are an informed customer with an interest in your own health; second, the more information you have, the more confident you can feel.

Choose the questions most important to you from the following list. Check the ones you want. Since time might be limited with the doctor, identify your top five and mark them A or #1. The find the second most important and mark them with a B or #2. If you are optimistic, pick a third group. Set your priorities. Take this book with you and read from your list. Not all of the questions will apply to your situation, especially if you're having an outpatient procedure.

Take a friend who can take notes, or at least a tape recorder. Meetings with surgeons are notorious for bringing on amnesia. We are all nervous about surgery and about meeting doctors. What did the doc actually say? Best: a friend taking notes AND a tape recorder.

First Questions

The most immediate things you want to know, right off, are answers to this first group of questions, intended for your first meeting, when you are considering an operation for the first time. If you already know this material, feel free to move to the second set.

___ **What operation are you recommending? What does it involve?**

During your session with the surgeon, ask for an explanation of what's going on in your body and how the surgical procedure usually goes. If, for example, an organ has to be repaired or removed, why is it necessary? Your surgeon can use illustrations or models to explain to you the steps involved in the procedure. There are often different ways of performing the same operation. One way may require more extensive surgery than another. You need to understand which method your surgeon will be adopting, and why your surgeon prefers one procedure over another.

___ **Why do I need the operation?**

Make sure you understand how the proposed operation fits in with the diagnosis of your medical condition.

___ **When do I need the operation? Is it urgent?**

You need to know if there is some flexibility in the timing. Is the timing for your benefit?

___ **Are there alternatives to surgery?**

Surgery is not always the only solution to a problem. Medical therapy or other non-surgical treatments, such as a change in diet or special exercises, might help you as much as surgery, or more. Ask your surgeon and primary care doctor about the benefits and risks involved in the other choices. You need to know as much as possible about these benefits and risks in order to make the most appropriate decision.

___ **What are the benefits of undergoing the operation?**

Ask your surgeon what you will gain by undergoing the operation. For example, a hip joint replacement could mean that you can walk again with ease. Also, ask how long the benefits of surgery are likely to last.

___ **What are the risks of undergoing the operation?**

All operations carry an element of risk, which is why you need to carefully weigh the benefits of the operation against the risks of complications or side effects.

___ **What could happen if I don't have this operation, or if I delay it?**

Ask your surgeon what you will gain—or lose—by not undergoing the operation immediately. Could you develop more pain? Could your condition get worse? Could the problem go away? Getting a second opinion from another doctor is a very good way of making sure that undergoing the operation is the best alternative for you. If you are seeking a second opinion, make sure to get your records from the first doctor so that the second one does not have to repeat the tests.

___ **Would you tell me about the surgery? Where and how big is the incision? How will it be closed? Do I stay in the hospital?**

You may have a preference, say, for stitches over staples. At some point you need to find out whether you'll need to be hospitalized. You probably won't need to ask, though, as it is one of the first things doctors tell you.

___ **How many surgeries of this type have you done?**

Outcomes are better when the surgeon has done many.

___ **How many surgeries of this type have been done at this hospital?**

Studies show that the highest percentages of success happen where the hospital has done many of the same type. If the hospital has done many, but the surgeon only a few, the hospital's experience improves your doctor's success rate. If there's a chance to choose, go to the hospital that has solid experience in your condition. It's not just the doctors, but the collective experience of the staff regarding the operation itself, recovery, proper medication for your situation, and possible complications.

Questions When You Are Already Scheduled For Surgery

Choose those most important to you and make a check mark by them. You won't have time to ask everything.

___ **What will my recovery look like? How much time is involved? What help will I need?**

Patients are often able to leave the hospital sooner than a few years ago. Many surgeries that once required a stay are now short stay, or outpatient. The good part is that a shorter stay means less time for some germ to get you and less expense. On the other hand, you might need more help at home.

___ I'd like to have Healing Statements said out loud during the procedure. Will you say them to me, or should Dr. _____ (the anesthesiologist) say them?

Show what you'd like said, and ask for help. The healing statements are in Chapter 6, along with the instructions. Most surgeons will go along with this even if they don't fully believe it has an effect. Some will say it can't hurt. That's OK, as long as they agree to do it. It seems to work even when the doctor's belief is weak. Actually, the anesthesiologist is often the one to say the words, and might be even more into it. See below for anesthesiologist questions.

___ Will you ask everyone in the Operating Room to speak and act as if I were awake, hearing every word, and in a suggestible state?

You really do hear what is said under anesthesia. Doctors and nurses used to think that they could say anything, but it has turned out that patients can recall every word later in hypnosis. The words that are spoken have an effect, for good or ill, on your outcome and recovery.

___ Will you make a picture for me of how my _____ will look when it is healed?

This is so you can visualize your healing. A drawing, even a rough sketch, is enough for your imagination to work with.

___ Can I have control over my pain medication after surgery?

It feels reassuring to many of us to have some control over our own analgesia. There is usually some pain after surgery. It would be prudent to find out how much you may have and what the doctors and nurses will do to reduce it. Controlling the pain will help you become more comfortable during recuperation, which will help you to recover faster.

___ Can we talk about what will happen if you find something during the operation?

This question does not apply to all operations. If it does for you, and if you are concerned about the surgeon finding something bad, tell her or him straight out that you would appreciate not hearing about it during or immediately after surgery, but later, when you are relatively stable and comfortable.

___ How is infection controlled in surgery and in my room?

It's good to hear that the hospital is active and concerned. Affirm to yourself: "The hospital and staff are doing a great job in taking care of me, and my immune system is strong."

___ **Tell me about catheter sterilization** (if it applies)

Same. You want to know they're thinking about it.

___ **Will there be any problem having one of my Support Team present in my room at all hours?**

Only applies if you're staying overnight. You are entitled to this by law, but it's good to ask anyway, so there will be no surprises. Your friends can help make sure hands are washed, your sleep is not interrupted unnecessarily, and medications are correct.

___ **Will someone try to wake me up in the middle of the night?**

In the first day or so after surgery, or with some illnesses, it might be necessary. The idea is to eliminate unnecessary awakenings, which interfere with your healing system's abilities to repair you. Ask for an explanation.

___ **How can I make sure that I won't get unnecessary or conflicting medications, or dosage errors?**

Get your medications written down so you or your Support Team can make sure you're getting what you are supposed to be getting. If there is a change, you want to know. Tape the list to your hospital gown as well.

___ **How can I avoid all but the most necessary tests and procedures?**

This will not apply if you won't be staying overnight. Get an idea of what the surgeon believes will be necessary. Your Support Team helper can check to see if tests are on the list.

___ **I'd like to have a tape (or CD) player and headphones during surgery. OK?**

If you are having a head operation, this may not be easy, which makes the Healing Statements said by the doctors even more important. Otherwise, you ought to be able to listen.

___ **Will you give me a referral for a Therapeutic Touch or hypnosis before and soon after the operation?**

All are very helpful in your recovery, as are other forms of energy work. See the Support Team chapter for discussion. In many hospitals, you need a written order from the doctor. Therapeutic Touch and its relatives ease and speed wound and injury healing. Believe me. You want this.

___ I have here the vitamins I am taking and plan to take afterwards. Will there be any problem about any of them? Do I need a note from you to show staff?

This applies only if you are staying overnight. Ideally, you have brought your vitamins in original bottles. A list is a poor second, but better than nothing.

___ When can I drink water? Eat solid food?

___ What medicines or supplements should I be taking, or not taking, in the time before surgery? And after?

Some medicines may have to be stopped. In some cases, you should not have aspirin, cold remedies, or other over-the-counter drugs without approval from your doctor.

___ What exercise should I do or not do before and after?

Exercise builds strength for healing for some patients, but may not be right for other people and conditions.

When Your Child Is Having Surgery: Additional Considerations

___ Can we arrange that my child not hear the words of the consent agreement out loud?

Children are in a highly suggestible state around surgery and hospital. Consider that everything they hear is a form of hypnotic suggestion that their subconscious minds will take as true. Let them hear only positive, encouraging, words.

___ Can I be present for my child's anesthesia? And go into the Operating Room with my child? And be present when he/she wakes up?

It's frightening enough for adults to be in the surgical process, but a child can feel especially alone and frightened. Administration of anesthesia is something to have worked out with the anesthesiologist at your meeting.

___ How can I make sure my child will get correct doses of medications?

Correct doses of correct meds are even more important than in adults, yet dosage errors are more frequent than with adults. I suggest taping a list to the hospital gown.

___ **How can we avoid an Adverse Drug Reaction?**

As you have read in Chapter 3, children are at greater risk for Adverse Drug Reactions. Take this opportunity to find out what medications are proposed and whether they are safe for children in those dosages.

___ **If you will use medications that are approved for adults, but not tested for children, how confident do you feel?**

Most medications used for children have not, in fact, been tested on children or approved for use on children. Most of the time, it works, but given the record of wrong dosages for children discussed in Chapter 3, keep it in mind. This is the biggest concern for children.

___ **Would you prescribe antibiotics for a cough, cold, bronchitis, or upper respiratory infection?**

If yes, ask them not to unless it's serious and they are certain the antibiotic is effective against the particular germs. Antibiotics are not effective for the vast majority of those conditions and you can prove it. See Chapter 3 for more information.

Questions for the Anesthesiologist

Arrange to see your anesthesiologist (the one who will be with you in the OR, if possible) at or near the same time as the pre-op meeting with the surgeon, if you can manage it. The value of an early meeting has been demonstrated in improved recovery times, shorter hospital stays and fewer complications. It needn't take a long time, just enough so you feel OK about what's happening. The anesthesiologist's position, often by your head, makes him or her the one person who has the best access to your ear and inner self.

Once again, I'll emphasize that by engaging directly with the doctor as a whole person, you automatically raise the level of caring about you. I recommend that you tell yourself that you are grateful for, and appreciative of, what they are doing for you. Go ahead and tell them that, but even if you are only feeling and thinking it, they can sometimes feel it. Look for a caring presence that you feel safe with. It's a real plus to have the person who so closely monitors your life signs actually know you and care about you as an individual. Let me say again: if possible, you want to meet the anesthesiologist who will be with you in surgery, not a supervisor or someone filling in.

___ Would you describe briefly what's going to happen?

This gives the doc a chance to give you the basic info and see how you respond. If you want lots of medical details, say so. Otherwise, ask for the outline and then ask about anything that isn't clear. If you have concerns, fears, or unpleasant memories, tell the doctor about them.

___ May I tell you now about medications I am taking (and/or known intolerances)?

Even though the info is probably on your paperwork, it's a good idea to bring it up. It makes a difference in the doctors' attitude toward you when you show a high level of interest in your own well-being. It is in your best interest to have two copies with you of your list of everything you are taking, one for your surgeon and one for the anesthesiologist.

___ What will you say to me as I enter the anesthetic state?

Here's a chance to talk over what you'd like to hear. Tell the doc what words or images make you feel safe and protected. Ask for help so you hear only positive speech from others in the Operating Room. Notice I didn't say, "go under" the anesthetic. As an empowered customer, you are entitled to enter a state of consciousness of your own free will. No need to feel "under" it. The anesthetic is your ally, too.

___ Will you hold my hand (or whatever gesture you prefer) as I go into anesthesia?

Discuss what sort of caring gesture might make you feel good. Most anesthesiologists are willing.

___ I want to use a healing (or relaxing) tape (or CD) and earphones. Can you help me with that?

You might need a little help. It's good to know for sure you'll have it.

___ I'd like to hear certain Healing Statements during and near the end of the surgery. Will you say them for me?

If they are familiar with the concept, they'll do it happily, because they'll know the information about improved surgical outcomes. Many anesthesiologists understand the reality of states of mind. They also know that your peace of mind makes their job less stressful—and that you'll probably require less anesthetic. This is the time to get it worked out. Hand him or her a copy of the statements from Chapter 6.

APPENDIX B
What to Bring to the Hospital

Here is a list of things to bring with you to the hospital in addition to your own personal list. A lot depends on how long you'll be in. You need a few more things for a longer stay, very few for a short stay. Check off what you need

—Personal Tape or CD player with headphones.
—Two sets of batteries: one new in the player plus a spare set.
—Guided Imagery or Hypnosis tapes/CDs and relaxation music.
—Favorite tapes/CDs: music, comedy, drama, books on tape, whatever can focus your attention.
—Healing Statements written on two sheets of paper—one set to tape on your hospital gown, one to give the surgeon.
—Mister bottle with your choice of essential oils.
—Medication list: clearly printed list of every medication you take, plus what you have been prescribed but are not taking.
—Disinfectant hand wipes.
—Homeopathic remedies, as listed in Chapter 9.
—Sleep mask to keep out light for better sleep and naps.
—Earplugs, so hospital noise doesn't get through so much.
—Travel Pad and Travel Comforter.
—Far-infrared socks.
—A stone, amulet, charm or good luck piece.
—A few pictures of loved people, holy people and/or places.
And:
—Health plan card
—Robe
—Slippers
—Shorts or sweat pants
—Socks
—Toothbrush and toothpaste

—Personal care things
—Pen and paper or notebook
—Phone numbers
—Reading material

Note: Do not bring any valuables with you, such as large sums of money, jewelry (including rings) or cellular phones.

APPENDIX C
Resources

For efficiency, I have put all these links on my website, www.WellnessCoaching.net/links. You only need type in one web address and click on the links.

Aromatherapy

Jan Meredith's website is the place to look if you need any of the Young Living formulations or essential oils. They are very good, reliable, and easy to get.

http://janme.younglivingworld.com

Books

I recommend only a few books because I want keep things simple, wanting to turn you on to good things without the excess baggage of scholasticism.

—*Second Opinion: The Columbia Presbyterian Guide to Surgery,* by Eric Rose, MD.

Published in 2000, this is the definitive, up-to-date guide for anyone whose doctor has recommended surgery. The author is Chief of Surgery at his hospital. Explains every aspect of 45 surgeries, provides good questions to ask. This is the best available book explaining the strictly medical aspects.

—*Going Under: Preparing Yourself for Anesthesia: Your Guide to Pain Control and Healing Techniques,* by Monica Furlong, Elliot Essinan, 1993

The title is self-explanatory. Everything you could want to know

—*Second Opinion: Your Comprehensive Guide to Treatment Alternatives,* by Isadore Rosenfeld, MD. A human book filled with reassuring material. Out of print, but still available used through Amazon and at many public libraries.

—*Coping With an Organ Transplant: A Practical Guide to Undertaking,*

Preparing For, and Living with an Organ Transplant, by Elizabeth Parr, Janet Mize

This is a must-read for patient, family, and support team of transplant patients.

—*8 Weeks To Optimum Health*, by Andrew Weil

This is a good guide that seems to make possible pulling your life together in a straightforward way. It is easy to follow, as it starts with a few simple, doable, changes, and adds a few each week. If you want to make changes in your health and lifestyle, this is a good place to look.

—*Your Body's Many Cries for Water,* by F. Batmanghelidj, Global Health Solutions 1997

A sustained rant about water and how to help all sorts of conditions with enough of it; contains compelling descriptions of the mechanics of how water deprivation can promote specific illnesses and imbalances.

—*After Surgery, Illness, Trauma,* by Sara Regina Ryan

Wonderful book that offers real sweetness of point of view, opening up the emotional side of trauma and healing. Highly recommended as a companion. One of the best complementary healing books in print.

—*Prepare for Surgery, Heal Faster,* by Peggy Huddleston

The pioneer book in mind-body preparation for surgery. The program based on the book is being taught to hospital personnel all over the country and helping many patients.

—*The Mozart Effect,* by Don Campbell

Illumination about healing and self-healing with music and tone.

—*Toning: The Creative Power of the Voice,* by Laurel E. Keyes & Elizabeth Keyes

Children

Parents' anesthesia brochure online at: www.asahq.org/patientEducation/childanes.htm

Flower Remedies

These remedies are amazingly effective at helping us change quickly from an undesirable state of mind to a desirable one See www.PowerofFlowers.net. Isha Lerner does great phone consultations

General Surgery Information

www.yoursurgery.com has lots of info on all the technical aspects of surgery. Excellent descriptions of most common operations, with pictures.

Another good site is www.webmd.com.

Message from Water web site
www.adhikara.com/water.html

This site has fantastic dark field micrphotographs showing the power of thoughts, words and prayers to affect the structure of water. I found these pictures astonishing. See also the book of the same name.

Nutrition.

Since the resources and links change, all links to recommended items are at my site.

Prayer Requests and Lists
—Science of Mind World Ministry of Prayer
Free 24-hr. prayer service
USA tel., calling within USA/Canada: 800-421-9600
USA tel., calling from all other countries: 720-904-8156
Web site: www.wmop.org/prayer.htm
—Silent Unity
Free 24-hr. prayer service USA telephone: 816-969-2000 (If you have no means of paying for the call: USA telephone. 800-669-7729); USA telephone Español: 816-969-2020; USA Telecom device for the deaf: 816-525-1155; Web site: www.unityworldhq.org/silent_unity.htm
—Christian
www.aconstantprayer.com
www.aprayer.net
www.upperroom.org/prayer_center/
www.americancatholic.org
www.prayerline.com
www.prayerrequestsite.com
www.salvationarmy-usaeast.org/spiritual/prayer/prayer_request.htm
—Other
—Prayer site of the Mystic World Fellowship: www.yogaworld.org/pray/

—Healing Buddha Foundation, Segyu Gaden Dhargye Ling: www.healingbuddha.org/pujas.asp

Recordings: Hypnosis and Guided Imagery

—*Successful Surgery*, Belleruth Naparstek. A pre-surgery session, a pre-surgery session with affirmations, and two tracks of relaxing, no-stress music. I used these while on the gurney before surgery. I couldn't have headphones on because it was eye surgery. Otherwise I would have. www.healthjourneys.com

—*Successful Surgery & Recovery*, Emmett Miller, MD. Two excellent tracks to get ready and two excellent tracks for recovery. I especially valued the recovery tracks. I liked having support for recovery.

—*Less Stress Surgery: A Guided Imagery Relaxation,* Neil Neimark, MD. One good session on both sides of the tape. Very specific instructions to the body based on recent research. He calls it guided imagery, as does Belleruth Naparstek, but they look, act, and sound like hypnosis to me.

—*Healing for Surgery*, Wendi Friesen. Side One is *Preparation for Surgery*. Side Two is *Rapid Healing after Surgery*. These are very good sessions and, as with Emmett Miller, I appreciated the recovery session.

Other Recordings

—*Healing Yourself With Your Own Voice* (audiotape), by Don Campbell

—*Pain Control*, from The Monroe Institute. Special frequencies and hemi-synch technology to organize brain waves. Very effective.

—*Surgery Set*, from the Monroe Institute.

Sleep

One of the best things I have found for people who have a history of not sleeping well, including me, is the Nikken Sleep System. If you are already thinking of changing your bed, give it a long look. I believe it helped me move quickly from chronic exhaustion to being well rested and energetic. Indications are that people get more deep sleep on the system. Contact a Nikken consultant or email me through my site.

A very good hypnosis tape/CD is *Deep Sleep Every Night*, from Diviniti Publishing in England.

APPENDIX D
Guided Imagery Before Surgery Script

You can record this script for yourself or have a friend read it aloud to you while you are in a comfortable position. Let me remind you that many effective scripts, including this one, may seem odd on paper, but can be very effective when spoken. This one has in it the elements shown by research to be the most useful. Try it. When you see three dots (…), pause and take a breath. If you like the earlier short script in Chapter 7, called "Imagining Excellent Recovery", feel free to add it onto this one. You can also add in some or all of the Healing Statements from Chapter 6.

SCRIPT: Preparing For A Surgical Procedure

Take a nice long slow deep breath in and slowly breathe out…Relax now. Again, take a long slow, deep breath in…and out…Relax now… Take another slow deep breath…in…and out…Relax now…The next time you exhale, your eyes close naturally…and you feel the relaxation in your eyelids, so relaxed…you wouldn't even want to open them. Now let that relaxation spread from your eyelids to the top of your head and feel it ripple down your body to the tips of your toes.

Notice how relaxed you are now. Let each and every easy breath relax you more…The sound of my voice is relaxing, relaxing is a pleasure, as you drift deeper and deeper into a pleasant, easy state.

You notice the feel of your thighs resting on the chair or bed where your body makes contact, notice the feel of your back…your arms… making contact…As you notice the temperature of the air on your skin…you feel safe and secure…

To help you go even deeper into this quiet relaxed state, I ask you now to imagine yourself standing comfortably on the upper level of a terraced garden, a very pleasant garden…feeling safe and secure…and when I begin counting, I'll ask you to begin descending…ten steps down…to the lower level of this beautiful garden…Standing now on the top of the staircase of relaxation...Begin to descend now...(*Note: take 5-10 seconds for each step down)

Ten...starting down...

Nine.... with each step down, you are doubling your level of relaxation...

Eight.... letting go of all worldly cares for now...

Seven.... deeper and deeper relaxed

Six.... feeling safe and secure...deeper inside now...

Five.... pause a moment...and you might feel a supportive presence around you, a healing presence...your inner healer...perhaps you can see, or feel, a helpful figure...a person...an angel...it doesn't matter, just so you feel the love and support as you take a step down, to...

Four.... calm and cared for

Three.... letting go, going deeper...

Two.... deeper and deeper...your helper is watching over you...

One.... very deeply relaxed...as you step into the beautiful garden, you notice a lake...there is a pleasant gentle breeze, you can hear tiny waves lapping at the shore as you gaze out over the lake. It is your lake of peace...The waves have a rhythm; they calm and relax you...You notice a very comfortable-looking reclining chair on the shore and you relax into its soft, warm comforting surface...gazing casually at the lake...and you feel very good...you know you can return here before and during your operation, or any other time...

Lying comfortably in this safe place, at ease, feeling the presence of your inner healer, you drift into a dreamy state...and imagine yourself entering the hospital...Say to yourself, "This is where my body is going to be repaired so it can get well...so I can help my doctor help me to wellness...I have decided that this procedure will bring my body to wellness...The surgeon and staff are here to help me...We are all cooperating...We are a team...we work together...Imagine yourself in your hospital gown, calm and relaxed, in an area where you are waiting before the operation. The preparatory procedures are happening easily and you remain at peace. Your inner healer is with you.

Now imagine the scene changing to the room where the procedure is to take place.... You are feeling relaxed and confident...Notice how much more relaxed you are...You are doing fine. The doctor is there to help you repair your body so that you can have wellness and peace of mind...You can hear sounds around you, but you pay no attention to them unless your name is spoken by the doctor...addressing you directly, perhaps saying your Healing Statements. The other sounds in the room just pass you by, relaxing you even more.

Imagine friends, family, support team, with you in spirit, joining your inner healer, wishing you well...Perhaps you hear their voices, perhaps you feel a presence, or even see them, as their presence helps relax your body so the anesthetic you receive is taken in easily...In fact you need only a small amount of anesthetic, because your body is cooperating so well...You are in control of what's happening to your body. During the procedure, your body knows how to remain as deeply anesthetized as it needs to be for your comfort and safety. Your anesthesiologist is looking after you, carefully monitoring your signs...You have set the processes into motion through your ability to relax on command, your own command...Every time you hear the phrase, "You are doing fine," all of your healing systems come together to function in a normal healthy manner...They create complete recovery within and without...

Relax and take a nice easy deep breath...Your lungs breathe freely, filling your body with healthy air, sending healing nutrients to every part of you.

Your body already knows how to relax the muscles all around the incision...your body knows to relax to allow the doctor to work easily... your body knows to allow the whole area to remain comfortable, feeling safe and secure, knowing the outcome is very good...

Your body knows to allow the blood to remain away from the site when the incision is open, allowing just enough moisture to allow the doctor to work easily...Your body knows how to cooperate with this procedure.... When the procedure is over, your muscles will be relaxed and loose, easily allowing blood to return to the area, bringing all the healing elements, oxygen, nutrients, antibodies, to speed your recovery. When the doctor indicates the procedure is over, this life-giving blood flows in to heal your surgery site, bringing natural pain relievers, endorphins, allowing you, naturally, to remain comfortable...and heal so very well.

You are doing fine. Notice how good you feel about being in control of your thoughts and feelings...Each and every time you practice this, you become calmer and more relaxed...

Now imagine yourself in your chair back at the lakeshore…and you feel calm and relaxed as you look out onto the calm waters…Calm and relaxed…. Enjoying the scene that is before you…smelling the aromas and scents of nature, enjoying the sun on the water…Calm and relaxed…Your healing figure is with you, taking care, looking out for you. Notice the feeling of knowing that you are looked after…Your body cooperates with the skillful hands of the surgeon. It has only the exact amount of blood flow necessary to maintain perfect balance…In fact your body knows exactly what to do, and it does it in perfect cooperation with the surgeon…All of your vital signs are in perfect order; blood pressure perfect, heart rate perfect, breathing normal. You are enjoying your time at the lake, calm…and relaxed…calm and relaxed. You are doing fine…

From the moment that you decided to have this surgery done, your body began the healing process…Your body knows just what to do in order to get you to wellness. Your healing system is in gear, your immune system is functioning strongly, and everything about you is cooperating with your medical team…They are *your* medical team, and you are in charge. They are doing the work that is theirs to do, while your healing system and immune system are doing their work, everyone cooperating…All of your blood cells are doing their jobs perfectly. Imagine your medical team working well together, skillfully, being highly satisfied that this operation is one of the best they've done…. because your healing system is cooperating fully. You are doing fine.

After the procedure is over, it is easy for you to allow your stomach to feel a natural sense of hunger, even to growl a little…And you think of the foods you love, what you most desire to eat, because normal healthy eating leads to normal healthy elimination, letting you return home sooner in greater health and comfort. And you instruct your body to produce the natural chemicals that gently return your stomach and intestines to normal activity, taking in nutrients from the healthy foods you'll be able to eat with delight. As you desire your favorite foods, you feel a gentle warmth return to your stomach, blood flowing and intestinal activity returning, and it feels good to you.

And at the same time, another of your body's wonderful abilities follows your lead: you call upon your adrenal glands to rest easy…and you give them a signal here now…to relax and gently moderate their activity after the operation…allowing more healing white blood cells and life-affirming antibodies to move to the area...and you allow the repairs that your body knows, so well, how to do, and especially well when you are feeling safe and secure, when you are feeling in control, as you are right now.

Take a few moments to let these suggestions work in your subconscious mind (30 seconds). You are doing fine. When it is time, when the procedure is complete...and not before...you witness yourself come to full consciousness in the recovery area...Notice how relaxed and comfortable you feel. You have an appetite and are eager to eat small amounts of food, easily and effortlessly. You find that you are thirsty and drink water easily. Your bladder and bowel can work easily and appropriately. All of your organs are functioning normally and naturally. You feel wonderful, like you have had a magical summer nap in your reclining chair at the lake. You are doing fine...You have an awareness that a procedure has taken place. You are comfortable and full of energy...You are in control and healing has begun and will continue...It is now time to thank your inner healer, family, and friends, for being with you...I'll give you time to do that now...(30 sec).

Imagine, feel the love and support that you have around you and know that it is with you before, during and after the procedure...as it is now. Perhaps you hear the voices of your friends, family, Support Team, those who love you and care about you, welcoming you home. You can feel the warmth, you can see them caring for you...and you accept it, you let it in, knowing you have done everything possible to allow your body to heal safely and speedily...And you feel your healthy new tissues mending, healing, and strength returning to your body, knowing that your body will function with greater strength...and greater health...and greater peacefulness as it heals quickly.

You are already healing so well...Notice how good you feel...and continue to feel. Your recovery happens rapidly, easily and effortlessly... even better than you or your doctor expected.

In a moment, I will count to three...When I say "three," you will open your eyes and return to full social awareness...One, getting ready to come back from the lake...(10 seconds) two, nearly here...(10 seconds) and THREE. Open your eyes now, feeling good, refreshed, alive, knowing that you have created a healing for yourself.

NOTES

Introduction
1. Carol Norred, RN, "Minimizing Preoperative Anxiety with Alternative Caring-Healing Therapies"; *American Organization of Registered Nurses Journal* (AORN), 11/1/2000
2. Christiane Northrup, MD; *Women's Bodies, Women's Wisdom;* Bantam Revised Edition March 1998, pp. 658 ff.

Chapter 1: Your Medical Team
1. Norman Cousins, *Head First: The Biology of Hope*, Dutton 1989, p. 258
2. Marc Darrow, M.D., medical director of the Joint Rehabilitation and Sports Medical Center (www.jointrehab.com), a holistic healing center in Los Angeles. Quoted in: "Back In Business: Surgery Isn't Always the Spinal Answer;" *Los Angles Magazine*, 3/01/02, by Jenna McCarthy.
3. Quoted in Norman Cousins, p.122
4. *New York Times*, 10/01/02, page D6, citing study in British Medical Journal of 9/27/02)
5. Favorable outcomes from meeting the doctors. L.D. Egbert, ,G.E. Battit, C.E. Welch, and M.K. Bartlett; "Reduction of Post-operative Pain by Encouragement and Instruction of Patients." *New England Journal of Medicine* 270 (1964); 25-27
6. Cousins, p. 44
7. Judith Petry, MD, *"Surgery and Complementary Therapies: A Review"*; in *Alternative Therapies in Health and Medicine,* 200;6(5):64-74 and at Dr. Petry's website, www.sover.net//~jpetry/essay/Surgery&Comp.htm
8. *Timeless Healing*, Herbert Benson MD, with Marg Stark. Scribner 1993, p. 103. Citing study by Dr David Eddy of the Jackson Hole Group
9. Benson, p.237: 72% of patients do not tell their doctors about unconventional treatments and remedies they are using.
10. Benson, p. 32
11. Benson, p. 37
12. Benson, p. 38

Chapter 2: Your Personal Support Team

1. Dartmouth study cited by Benson, p. 180

2. Dean Ornish, MD, quoted in Bill Moyers, *Healing and the Mind*, Doubleday, A Main Street Book, 1995, p. 31

3. William S. Harris, PhD; Manohar Gowda, MD; Jerry W. Kolb, MD; et al. "A Randomized, Controlled Trial of the Effects of Remote, Intercessory Prayer on Outcomes in Patients Admitted to the Coronary Care Unit;" Archives of Internal Medicine, 1999;159: 2273-2278 Vol. 159 No. 19, October 25, 1999

4. "The efficacy of 'distant healing': a systematic review of randomized trials;" Astin JA et al., *Annals of Internal Medicine* 132(11): 903-10. Jun 2000.

5. John Travis, MD, in his Introduction to *After Illness, Surgery, Trauma*, by Sara Regina Ryan, p. xv, Holm Press, 2000

6. Christiane Northrup, MD; *Women's Bodies, Women's Wisdom;* p. 669.

7. "Effect of Non-contact Therapeutic Touch on the Healing Rate of Full Thickness Dermal Wounds;" Scientific abstract by Daniel P. Wirth, M.S., J.D (at http://www.issseem.org/V1N1Abs.html)

"The effect of Non-Contact Therapeutic Touch (NCTT) on the rate of surgical wound healing was examined in a double-blind study. Full-thickness dermal wounds were incised on the lateral deltoid region using a skin punch biopsy instrument, on healthy subjects randomly assigned to treatment or control groups. Subjects were blinded both to group assignment and to the true nature of the active treatment modality in order to control placebo and expectation effects. Incisions were dressed with gas-permeable dressings, and wound surface areas were measured on Days 0, 8, and 16 using a direct tracing method and digitization system. Active and control treatments were comprised of daily sessions of five minutes of exposure to a hidden Therapeutic Touch practitioner or to sham exposure. Results showed that treated subjects experienced a significant acceleration in the rate of wound healing as compared to non-treated subjects at day seven."

8. "Researchers Learn How Stress Slows Wound Healing;" *Science Daily,* July 28, 1999

Source: Ohio State University. Article at: www.sciencedaily.com/releases/1999/07/990728073743.htm

9. Smith, MC et al, "Benefits of massage therapy for hospitalised patients: a descriptive and qualitative evaluation;" *Alternative therapies in Health and Medicine* 5(4): 64-71, Jul 1999.

10. Kim MS et al, "Effects of hand massage on anxiety in cataract surgery using local anesthesia;" *Journal of Cataract and Refractive Surgery*, 27 (6): 884-90. Jun 2001

11. Carol Norred, RN, "Minimizing Preoperative Anxiety with Alternative Caring-Healing Therapies"; *AORN Journal*, 11/1/2000)

12. Wardell DW, Engebretson J. "Biological correlates of Reiki Touch (sm) healing;" *Journal of Advanced Nursing* 33 (4): 439-45; Feb 2001.

13. From the Emotional Freedom Technique web site, www.emofree.com

14. The significant decrease of the resistive index during reflexology demonstrates a decrease of flow resistance in kidney vessels and an increase of renal blood flow. These results are consistent with the hypothesis that organ-associated reflexology is effective in changing renal blood flow during therapy. Sudmeier I. et al. "Changes of renal blood flow during organ-associated foot reflexology measured by color Doppler sonography;" *Forschende Komplementaermedizin* 6(3): 129-34 Jun 1999.

Chapter 3: Hospital Risk Factors and How to Minimize Them

1. Ron Anderson MD, in Bill Moyers, *Healing and the Mind*, p. 31

2. *Surgery: A Patient's Guide from Diagnosis to Recovery*, by Claire Mailhot RN, Melinda Brubaker RN, Linda Garrett Slezak RN; UCSF Nursing Press 1999, p xv.

3. Pneumonia accounts for 15% of all hospital-acquired infections. It's the second most frequent hospital infection after urinary tract infections, which make up 34% of the total. The incidence of nosocomial pneumonia is about 6 per 1000 hospitalized patients. In the US, 200,000 people acquire infections from intravascular catheters each year and nearly a million people suffer urinary-tract infections from urinary catheters. (Fourth Decennial International Conference on Nosocomial and Healthcare-Associated Infections, *MMWR,* February 25, 2000 / 49(07); 138). The same data can be found in: DiPiro JT, Martindale RG, Bakst A, Vacani PF, Watson P, Miller MT, "Infection in surgical patients: effects on mortality, hospitalization, and postdischarge care. *Am J Health Syst Pharm* 1998 Apr 15; 55(8):777-81)

One study, done with hidden cameras, showed that doctors wash their hands less than half the time they are supposed to. What about rubber gloves? Aren't they supposed to reduce cross-contamination? Unfortunately, the study goes on to say, transmission of infection has been reported even with use of gloves, and comes from either breaks in the glove or the omission by health care workers to change their gloves between contacts with different patients. Hospitals are busy. Nurses and doctors say that they are overwhelmed. They might see a hundred patients in a day and can't wash 100 times. "Handwashing: A modest measure with big effects;" *Handwashing Liaison Group. BMJ* 1999; 318: 686-686 (13 March)

"Bacteria responsible for the infections are found everywhere in the hospital and are frequently spread from patient to patient through contaminated hands of health care workers. The risk of spreading the infection could be considerably reduced by adhesion to simple handwashing practices. However, doctors often do not comply with this practice, and as a consequence the use of gloves has been promoted in order to reduce cross-contamination. Unfortunately, transmission of infection has been reported even with use of gloves, and is attributable to either breaks in the glove, or to the omission by health care workers to change their gloves between contacts with different patients." "Guidelines for Prevention of Nosocomial Pneumonia;" *MMWR* January 03, 1997 / 46(RR-1); 1-79

4. "Don't Become a Medical Blunder," by Stacey Bradford, *Consumer Action, Jan 31,2002*

5. Weber DJ, Raasch R, Rutala WA;, "Nosocomial infections in the ICU: the growing importance of antibiotic-resistant pathogens," *Chest* 1999 Mar;115(3 Suppl):34S-41S. "Measures of prevention include proper hand washing, patient isolation, proper disinfection and sterilization techniques, and judicious use of antibiotics, as demonstrated by the fact that hospitals with the highest rates of hospital-acquired infections also have the highest rates of antibiotic use."

6."Don't Become a Medical Blunder," by Stacey Bradford, *Consumer Action,* Jan 31,2002

7. Gonzales R, Steiner JF, Sande MA, "Antibiotic prescribing for adults with colds, upper respiratory tract infections, and bronchitis by ambulatory care physicians;" *Journal of the American Medical Association*

(*JAMA*), 1997 Sep 17; 278 (11):901-4. And: Metlay JP, Stafford RS, Singer DE, "National trends in the use of antibiotics by primary care physicians for adult patients with cough;" *Arch Intern Med* 1998 Sep 14;158 (16):1813

8. *JAMA*, Vol 284 July 26, 2000

9. A distressing number of physicians specializing in childcare prescribe the wrong dose of medication to infants and children. This finding is important, since inappropriate dosage in this age group may be associated with significant morbidity and mortality. Approximately 10% of residents who participated in this study committed a 10-fold dosage error, which may be life threatening. Rowe C; Koren T; Koren G., "Errors by pediatric residents in calculating drug doses;" *Arch Dis Child,* 79(1): 56-8 1998 Jul.

Also, Gonzalez-Martin G, Caroca CM, Paris E., "Adverse drug reactions (ADRs) in hospitalized pediatric patients. A prospective study;" *Int J Clin Pharmacol Ther* 1998 Oct; 36(10):530-3.

10. Mitchell AA, Goldman P, Shapiro S, Slone D, "Drug utilization and reported adverse reactions in hospitalized children;" *Am J Epidemiol* 1979 Aug;110(2):196-204

11. Extrapolation of these data to the entire U.S. population showed that in 1992, physicians wrote 6.5 million prescriptions for children with URTIs (Upper Respiratory Tract Infections) or common cold and 4.7 million prescriptions for children with bronchitis, despite the fact that, as emphasized in the article, antibiotic treatment is typically ineffective in these conditions. Nyquist AC, Gonzales R, Steiner JF, Sande M., "Antibiotic prescribing for children with colds, upper respiratory tract infections, and bronchitis;" *JAMA.* 1998 Mar 18; 279 (11):875-7

12. "Doctor Links Kids' Fears to Recovery," By Lauran Neergaard, AP Medical Writer Dec 9, 2002

13. A study involved the assessment of a variety of preoperative psychological supports aimed at reducing stress in pediatric patients and their parents. The conclusion was that preoperative discussion of the activities before and after surgery greatly lowered anxiety. Visintainer M, Wolfer J (1975); "The effect on children's and parents' stress responses and adjustment;" *Pediatrics,* 56, 187-202)

14. a) A study conducted on 157 hospital patients aged 70 and over showed that 14.6% of them experienced adverse drug reactions (ADRs),

that were potentially preventable in half the cases. Upon discharge, 50% of patients with ADRs experienced a decline in one or more activities of daily living, compared to 24% of patients without ADRs. See Gray SL, Sager M, Lestico MR, Jalaluddin M., "Adverse drug events in hospitalized elderly;" *J Gerontol A Biol Sci Med Sci* 1998 Jan;53(1):M59-63)

b) The results of a study, conducted on 315 elderly patients consecutively admitted to the hospital, show that in 28.2% of them, the cause of hospitalization was related to the medication they were taking, and was due to noncompliance with treatment in 11.4% of cases, and to adverse drug reactions in another 16.8%. Col N; Fanale JE; Kronholm P; "The role of medication noncompliance and adverse drug reactions in hospitalizations of the elderly." *Arch Intern Med,* 150(4): 841-5 1990 Apr.)

c) This study evaluated the rate of prescribing of drugs with absolute contraindications or which were unnecessary, in a sample population of 416 elderly patients consecutively admitted to a teaching hospital. On admission, 11.5% of patients were receiving drugs with absolute contraindications, and 27% were receiving drugs that were unnecessary. Adverse drug reactions (ADRs) occurred in 27% of patients on medication, and half of these reactions were due to drugs with absolute contraindications or unnecessary. ADRs were the cause of hospital admission in 6.3% of patients, and were due to inappropriate prescribing (and were therefore avoidable) in half of the cases. Lindley CM, et al "Inappropriate medication is a major cause of adverse drug reactions in elderly patients;" *Aging* 1992 Jul;21(4):294-300)

15. "Don't Become a Medical Blunder," by Stacey Bradford, *Consumer Action, Jan 31,2002.*

Chapter 4: Cultivating a Healing Point of View

1. Max Heindel (1865-1919), *Occult Principles of Health and Healing,* online at http://www.rosicrucian.com/oph/opheng01.htm

2. Jeanne Achterberg, *Imagery in Healing: Shamanism and Modern Medicine*, New Science Library, Shambala, 1985, p.172,

3. Herbert Benson, *Timeless Healing*, p 14

4. "Optimism is Associated With Mood, Coping, and Immune Change in Response to Stress" by Suzanne C. Segerstrom, Ph.D., Shelley E. Taylor, Ph.D., Margaret E. Kemeny, Ph.D., and John L. Fahey, Ph.D., University of California Los Angeles, in *Journal of Personality and Social Psychology*, Vol. 74, No. 6

5. Quoted in "A Bright Future for PNI," by Tori DeAngelis; *Monitor on Psychology,* Vol 33, June 2002

6. *Christianity Today,* October 4, 2001; "The Great Physician Is In" "Studying the benefits and perils of religious belief on physical health–including pregnancy:" Certain forms of religiousness may increase the risk of death. Elderly ill men and women who experience a religious struggle with their illness appear to be at increased risk of death, even after controlling for baseline health, mental health status, and demographic factors." Bowling Green State University Psychology professor Kenneth Pargament and others found that if sick people thought they were being abandoned or punished by God, that Satan caused their illness, or that they were being abandoned by their church, they were more likely to die. (Pargament presented much of the findings at the American Psychological Association convention in August 2000.)

7. Taylor, Kemeny, Reed, and colleagues, American Psychologist Vol 55 No. 1

8. "Healing and prayer: the power of paradox and mystery," Larry Dossey, MD; IONS *Review* (Institute of Noetic Sciences) #28 1993 Winter

9. Achterberg, pp 182-187.

10. Achterberg, p.187

11. Benson, p.30.

12. Achterberg, p.17

13. "Timeless Mind, Ageless Body," Deepak Chopra; *IONS Review* (Institute of Noetic Sciences), Vol. 28, Winter 1993, pp 16-21

14. "Studying For Surgery, Workshop addresses role of the mind in healing," York Daily Record, York PA, 12/22/2001

15. Law of Attraction is explained well by the group of spirits known as Abraham speaking through Esther Hicks. This material can be found at www.abraham-hicks.com.

16. From Stephen Levine, "Conscious Living/Conscious Dying", Thinking Allowed Productions, an Interview at www.thinkingallowed.com/levine.html

17. Abraham, from www.abraham-hicks.com

18. John Zawacki, MD, quoted in Bill Moyers, *Healing and the Mind,* p. 147

Chapter 5: Breathing and Relaxation

1. "Researchers Learn How Stress Slows Wound Healing", *Science Daily,* July 28, 1999

Source: Ohio State University. Article at: www.sciencedaily.com/releases/1999/07/990728073743.htm

The article continues: "'But the analysis showed that women who had reported more stress before the experiments produced significantly lower levels of both cytokines,' Kiecolt-Glaser said. 'Those same women showed higher levels of the hormone cortisol in their saliva. Cortisol plays an important role in curtailing the healing process—higher cortisol levels can lead to a slowdown in healing.'

'When we looked at the levels of cortisol in the saliva and compared them to the levels of both cytokines, we saw the kind of correlation we would expect if the immune response was being affected,' explained William Malarkey, professor of internal medicine and director of GCRC. Malarkey said that normally, when levels of cortisol increase, it suppresses the immune response. It either reduces the number of neutrophils that rush to the wound site or it controls the concentration of the cytokines necessary for healing.

'It's important to note that the women in this experiment were really average in terms of the stress they were experiencing,' Kiecolt-Glaser said. 'So this doesn't require desperate, terrible stress levels to see effects on the immune system.' Kiecolt-Glaser said that patients anticipating surgery probably have stress levels much higher and therefore, are at greater risk when it comes to proper wound healing. And people suffering from clinical depression are probably at much higher risks of poor healing."

2. www.mercola.com

3. From *Nature Cure, Philosophy & Practice Based on the Unity of Disease & Cure* Henry Lindlahr, M.D. Published by The Nature Cure Publishing Company, Chicago. Twentieth Edition, 1922

4. www.mercola.com

5. From www.askdrweil.com

6. Benson, *Timeless Healing,* pp 146-147

7. Benson, *Timeless Healing,* p 136

Chapter 6: The Power of Words to Boost Your Healing System

1. "The Nocebo Effect: Placebo's Evil Twin," by Brian Reid, at

Dr. Joseph Mercola's site, www.mercola.com/2002/may/18/placebo_nocebo.htm; originally from The Washington Post April 30, 2002; Page HE01

2. I recommend a visit to abraham-hicks.com for a great point of view on life and wellness.

3. www.abraham-hicks.com.

4. Peggy Huddleston, *Prepare for Surgery, Heal Faster, A Guide of Mind-Body Techniques*, Angel River Press, 1996, p 144; www.healfaster,com

5. Huddleston, p 161

Chapter 7: Imagery, Imagination and Hypnotherapy

1. This information is available in greater detail at Belleruth Naparstek's magnificent website, www.healthjourneys.com

2. See www.healthjourneys.com

3. "Minimizing Postoperative Anxiety with Alternative Caring-Healing Therapies," Carol R. Norred; *AORN Journal* 11/1/2000)

4. Renzi C, Peticca L, Pescatori M. "The use of relaxation techniques in the perioperative management of proctological patients: preliminary results." *International Journal of Colorectal Disease* 2000 Nov 15 (5-6): pp. 313-316.

5. Ginandes C, Brooks P, Sando W, Jones C, Aker J. "Can Medical Hypnosis Accelerate Post-Surgical Wound Healing? Results of a Clinical Trial." *American Journal of Clinical Hypnosis*, 45:4, April 2003, pp. 333-351

6. Halpin LS, Speir AM, CapoBianco P, Barnett SD., "Guided imagery in cardiac surgery. Outcomes;" *Management & Nursing Practice*, 2002 Jul-Sep 6 (3): 132-7.

7. Montgomery GH, Weltz CR, Seltz M, Bovbjer DH. "Brief presurgery hypnosis reduces distress and pain in excisional breast biopsy patients." *International Journal of Clinical and Experimental Hypnosis*, 2002 Jan; 50(1): pp.17-32.

8. Manyande A, Berg S, Gettins D, Stanford SC, Mazhero S, Marks DF, Salmon P. "Preoperative rehearsal of active coping imagery influences subjective and hormonal responses to abdominal surgery." *Psychosomatic Medicine*. 1995: 57: 177-182.

9. Ashton C Jr, Whitworth GC, et al. "Self-hypnosis reduces anxiety following coronary artery bypass surgery. A prospective, randomized trial." *J. Cardiovascular Surgery* (Torino); 1997 Feb; 38(1): pp. 69-75.

10. Ginandes, C. *Alternative Thera. Health Med* 1999; 5(2): 67-75)

11. "Integration of Behavioral and Relaxation Approaches Into the Treatment of Chronic Pain and Insomnia," National Institutes of Health; Technology Assessment Conference Statement, October 16-18, 1995

12. Study by the United Medical and Dental Schools of Guy's and St. Thomas' Hospitals, London. Drs. Evans and Richardson; *Advances* Vol 5:4, p. 11, 1989

13. *Mind & Body* newsletter from Neil Neimark, MD, Summer 2002

Chapter 8: Prayer, Forgiveness and Gratitude

1. Cardiologist Mitchell Krucoff, MD and Susan Craven, Nurse Practitioner, From www.mercola,com

2. *Vegetarian Times*, 2/01/02, by Laura Flynn McCarthy

3. Quoted in *Vegetarian Times* article, cited above

4. Dr. Harold Koenig, quoted in *Vegetarian Times*

5. Rogerio Lobo, MD, Chairman of Gynecology and Obstetrics at Columbia University, *Christianity Today,* October 1, 2001. "The Great Physician Is In: Studying the benefits and perils of religious belief on physical health–including pregnancy."

6. From *Duck Soup for the Soul*, by Steve Bhaerman, professionally known as Swami Beyondananda, Sourcebooks, Naperville, IL, 1999; p.107. Reprinted with permission.

7. This explanation of prayer owes much to Abraham, whose work is spoken through Esther Hicks at www.abraham-hicks.com.

8. Quoted in Joan and Miroslav Borysenko, *The Power of the Mind to Heal*. Hay House. 1994, p. 196

9. "Giving up Grudges; Forgiveness eases anger and heartache," by Julie Sevrens,

5/25/99, *San Jose Mercury News*,

10. Benson, *Timeless Healing*. p. 10.

11. Quoted in "Forgive and your health won't forget," by Jane Lampman; Christian Science Monitor, 12/18/02

12. "Giving up Grudges," San Jose *Mercury News op. cit.*

13. Ibid

14. Psychic Betty Wall of Seattle, Washington, personal communication)

Chapter 9: Foods and Nutritional Supplements

1. Peltoh, Ross, "Speeding up Wound Healing: Health Benefits of Supplements;" *American Druggist*, Sept 1998. A link to the full text of this excellent article, which summarizes the science about the effect of each nutrient on surgical recovery, is at my web site at *www.wellnesscoaching.net/links*

2. Windsor, J. et al. "Wound healing Response in Surgery Patients," *British J Surgery* 75:135, 1988, cited in Peltoh.

3. The supplement suggestions are based on Surgery Recovery Programs By Robert M. Myers, ND, Alan R. Gaby, MD, Jonathan V. Wright, MD, at www.naturodoc.com, on the article cited above by Ross Peltoh, from the journal for pharmacists, American Druggist, Sept 1998, and on inspiration from Dr Saul at www.doctoryourself.com

4. From www.askdrweil.com, published 09/21/2000. There is considerable literature on the value of intravenous Vitamin C in surgery. At www.doctoryourself.com, there is an excellent article: "Observations On the Dose and Administration of Ascorbic Acid When Employed Beyond the Range Of A Vitamin In Human Pathology;" Frederick R. Klenner, M.D., F.C.C.P. Go read it all, but consider the following right away: First, after surgery, "...samples of blood taken six hours after surgery showed drops of approximately 1/4 the starting amount and at 12 hours the levels were down to one-half. Samples taken 24 hours later, without added ascorbic acid to fluids, showed levels 3/4 lower than the original samples." (Surgery causes major Vitamin C reduction in the body). However, "...normal wound healing may be produced by adequate vitamin C therapy during the post-operative period...Many other investigators have shown in both laboratory and clinical studies, that optimal primary wound healing is dependent to a large extent upon the vitamin C content of the tissues." See www.doctoryourself.com/strategies.html for a complete rundown on the science of both oral and intravenous Vitamin C

5. Peltoh, citing Phillips, JD, et al. "Effects of Chronic Corticosteroids and Vitamin A on the Healing of Intestinal Anastomoses," *Am J Surg* 163(1): 71-77, Jan 1992

6. Peltoh, citing Agren, MS, "Studies on Zinc in Wound Healing." *Acta Derm Venereol* Supp 154:1, 1990.

7. Barbul A, et al. "Arginine Enhances Wound Healing and

lymphocyte immune responses in humans;" *Surgery* 108(2): 331-336, Aug 1990, cited in Peltoh.

8. Okada, A, et al. "Zinc in Clinical Surgery: a research review." *Japanese Journal of Surgery* 20:635, 1990, cited in Peltoh

9. www.askdrweil.com

Chapter 10: The Value of Water

1. "Speeding up Wound Healing: health benefits of supplements, Ross Peltoh, *American Druggist,* Sept 1998

2. Barbara Levine, RD, PhD, is Director of the Nutrition Information Center at the New York Hospital—Weill Medical College of Cornell University. Source: www.water.com

Chapter 11: Protect Your Sleep

1. "The Slumber Solution," by Benedict Carey. *Health Magazine*, May 1996

2. Ibid.

3. Drs. Hughes and Singer at Oregon Health Sciences University, cited in Carey

4. Vitiello study, reported in Carey

5. *Proceedings* of the American Academy of Neurology's annual meeting in Denver, Colorado April 18, 2002; Presentation by Dr. Samir Bangalore from Northwestern University Medical School

6. The lecithin and L-tryptophan recommendations are at Dr. Saul's website, www.doctoryourself.com

Chapter 12: Music for Faster Recovery

1. Campbell, Don, *The Mozart Effect;* New York: Avon Books, 1997. Campbell explores the use of imagery and music with surgery, anxiolytic music, and music used during recovery from surgery. Guess what? Listening to music along with using imagery three days before surgery helps with postoperative recovery.

2. Godbey F, Wolfe L, "Sensory healing;" *Prevention*, 4, 24-25, (1997). This report involved colorectal surgery patients. It compared patients who listened to music tapes three days before surgery, during surgery, and after surgery, to those who did not listen to music. The results indicated that the listeners experienced half the postoperative anxiety and used half as much painkiller. Also, see Locsin, R. "The effect of music on the pain of selected post-operative patients," *Journal of Advanced Nursing, 6, 19-25,* 1981. The study looked at the effect of

music on patients during a two-day period after surgery and found that pain was decreased in the forty-eight hour period after surgery due to the use of music. Also, Merritt, R, "Giving good vibrations" *Inside DUMC,* 6, August 1997, from www2.mc.duke.edu/news/inside/970804/9.html. This pilot study at Duke looked at thirty-three patients undergoing knee replacement surgery. The study revealed that clients who listened to music before surgery decreased tension by twenty-one percent. Following surgery, less pain medication was used, and they left the hospital sooner. It proved to be a cost-effective therapy.

3. Heitz, L., Scamman F, Symreng T, "Effect of music therapy in the post anesthesia care unit [A nursing intervention];" *Journal of Post Anesthesia Nursing,* 7, 22-31, 1992. Studied the effect music had on pain and respiration in the Post Anesthesia Care Unit and the effect music had on patients' experience in the unit. There were three control groups. Group one did not wear headphones, group two wore headphones but heard no music, and group three wore headphones and listened to music. The results were that group three was able to wait much longer before requiring anesthesia and reported a consistently more pleasant experience from one day after surgery to one month.

4. Dean Evenson. Information at www.soundings.com/

5. Guzzetta CE, "Music therapy: Hearing the melody of the soul," in *Holistic Nursing: A Handbook for Practice,* third ed, B M Dossey, L Keegan, C E Guzzetta, eds; Gaithersburg, Md: Aspen Publishers, 2000, p. 587.

6. Koch ME et al, "The sedative and analgesic sparing effect of music," *Anesthesiology* 89 (August 1998) 300-306.

7. NIH National Institute of Nursing Research News Release, 5/10/99; Study led by Marion Good, PhD, RN, of Frances Payne Bolton School of Nursing, Case Western Reserve University.

8. University of Buffalo news release, 5/29/2001; study led by Karen Allen, Ph.D., research scientist in the UB Department of Medicine.

9. Rodgers L., "Music for surgery;" *Advances: The Journal for Mind, Body, Health,* 11, 49-58, 1995. Rodgers discusses patients' anxiety in the preoperative, intraoperative and postoperative period, finding that familiar music evokes too many memories and associations. The research reveals that melody can promote tension instead of relaxation, and that anxiolytic music (music avoiding songs, lyrics, singing or other tension), creates a free flow that allows patients to relax. Clinical outcomes indicate

that recordings are helpful before, during and after surgery. Linda Rodgers' work shows that patients do hear under anesthesia and that anxiolytic music does reduce anxiety. She recommends that audiotapes selected by each patient be played before, during, and after surgery on cassette (or CD) players with earphones. Another study looked at the effects of anxiolytic music on 97,000 patients, before, during, and after surgery, and 97% reported that music helped them relax during recovery. Soft tonal music was most effective.

Chapter 13: A Touch of Aromatherapy

1. *Complete Aromatherapy Handbook*, Suzanne Fischer-Rizzi, Sterling Publishing Co. NYC 1990, p. 26

2. Ibid, p. 27

3. *Orange County Register* online, 9/8/02:"Music, Aromatherapy put patients at ease during medical procedures"

4. S Jellinek, "Odours and mental states," *International Journal of Aromatherapy* 9 no. 3 (1999) 115-120.

5. M. Lis-Balchin, "Essential oils and aromatherapy: Their modern role in healing," *Journal of the Royal Society of Health* 117 (October 1997) 324-329

6. "Essential Oils and Hospital Germs," by Herve Chamus, MD, and "Statistical analysis of essential oils in gynecological infectious treatments," by Berangere Arnal-Schnebelen MD, found in *Integrated Aromatic Medicine 2000: Proceedings from the International Symposium*

7. Fischer-Rizzi, op. cit. p.94

8. Source: "Post-Surgical Swelling," By Dr. Andrew Saul at www.doctoryourself.com/vitamin_e.html

Chapter 14: Amazing Tools for Superior Healing

1. Vallbona C and Richards T., "Evolution of magnetic therapy from alternative to traditional medicine;" *Physical Medicine and Rehabilitation Clinics of North America.* 10(3): 729-54. Aug 1999. The authors, from Baylor College of Medicine, review the use of magnetic therapy in rehabilitation medicine (117 references). Static magnetic fields have been used for centuries to control pain and for other health problems, but only recently has scientific evidence regarding their efficacy been gathered in the West. The authors provide a historical review regarding the value of magnetic therapy in rehabilitation medicine. They also cover the modalities of magnetic therapy, biological effects of magnetic fields and the future of magnetic therapy.

2. Man D, Man B, Plosker H, "The influence of permanent magnetic field therapy on wound healing in suction lipectomy patients: a double-blind study;" J. Plast. Reconstr. Surg. 1999 Dec; 104(7): 2261-6

Made in United States
North Haven, CT
31 October 2024